The Kitchen Flowers

Volume 2

200+ *pasta* recipes:
Tips for a spacious kitchen

Debbie Brethold

LifeRich Publishing books may be ordered through booksellers or by contacting:

LifeRich Publishing
1663 Liberty Drive
Bloomington, IN 47403
www.liferichpublishing.com
844-686-9607

ISBN: 978-1-4897-4089-2 (sc)
ISBN: 978-1-4897-4090-8 (e)

Print information available on the last page.

LifeRich Publishing rev. date: 04/25/2022

LifeRich
PUBLISHING®

Thank you

Thank you to my mom and dad for their support, comments and enthusiastic responses through my culinary journey.

Thank you to my husband Richard for testing and tasting the recipes and also for his unfailing good humor.

Contents

Introduction
Cooking

For me cooking is about family, community and tradition. I was born and raised in St. Louis, Missouri. I absolutely love cooking. What I love most about cooking is the ability to be creative. It allows me to experiment with different cuisines and techniques. It also gives me the opportunity to learn about different cultures which are fascinating. I truly believe that anyone can cook and it can be fun and needed especially in the times we are in now. Being able to look in your pantry and create something out of what you have is just an incredibly satisfying feeling.

My mom set a good example about cooking when I was young. The kitchen was where we congregated as a family. She cooked almost daily and for the most part cooked with real ingredients. She wasn't inspired by someone else and got it done without a fuss when she did prepare a meal. I spent summers at my aunt's house where part of my daily chores included cooking. My aunt loved to eat and knew just what she wanted. I loved being her little helper and learned how to make her food just the way she liked it. Later in life I knew I wanted to be an entrepreneur of some sort. Writing, cooking, decorating, gardening, jewelry and amateur radio are my hobbies now. I decided to write cookbooks. I was curious about how I would achieve my goals and began writing. I had to find out what people liked to eat. I spent a lot of time in the kitchen preparing meals and critiquing them. The writing helped me. Cooking gave me a chance to be creative and also indulge in some play time with my family.

The Kitchen Flowers serves as the ideal kitchen companion when cooking. This beautiful volume is my first book to provide information about pasta, cooking oils and cooking tools. There are many other delights in the book. The unexpected recipe notes and wine pairings make a fun presence in the kitchen. These recipes are everything from Mediterranean pasta to Mexican pasta. While most of them are breezy and ideal for a Tuesday some are meant to cook on the rack beneath a main dish so they get done simultaneously. They can be a go to source for those looking for authentic Italian cooking. From exciting finds at the farmer's market to your own garden's bounty and even discoveries from your local grocery store these recipes and cooking tools will help you highlight the flavor for your fresh pasta dish. A dish doesn't need to require a lot of pans and tools to be downright delicious. Prepare them as is or change them and substitute lighter ingredients to suit your own taste or dietary needs.

Foreword

Healthy cooking oils

You should know that cooking should be done in oils much lower in saturated fats and trans fats. You will find that there are a variety of healthy oils to choose from each with its own purpose and star quality. There's so much more to the world of oils besides corn and canola. I've listed a few below.

Olive Oil: This is a green to yellow with infinite intermediate shades. The greener it is the fresher and the richer. Olive oil balances the acidity in high-acid foods such as tomatoes, vinegar and lemon juice and adds excellent depth to your salads. Drizzle it over salad or mix it into salad dressing and spruce up your greens and cooked pasta with oodles of health benefits.

Pumpkin Seed Oil: This is a dark green, tinged with red oil that is thick and fragrant. It's perfect in warm potato salad or drizzled over vegetables. Make sure to check the label before you buy to be sure you're getting 100% pumpkin seed oil and not something that's been blended with cheaper oils such as sunflower. This oil can't take high temperatures so don't use it as a replacement for oil when frying or sautéing. It will easily burn and valuable nutrients will be destroyed.

Hazelnut Oil: This is highly fragrant with a sweet, nutty taste (no surprises there). This light colored oil works well in dressings, marinades and baked goods. Its smoking point is fairly high so it can be used for general cooking. Like most oils it can go rancid so store it in the refrigerator or in a cool dark place at less than 65 degrees.

Walnut Oil: This is one of my favorite oils. The flavor is fantastic. It's expensive so I tend to use it sparingly. It is light in color, flavor and scent. It's not good for cooking due to its low smoking point and it'll go rancid over heat (a bitter taste reveals rancidity). It's best in cold dishes and is superb in dressings.

Avocado Oil: Another favorite. The best is cold pressed from the flesh of the avocado and most often comes from Australia and New Zealand. It is bright green, slightly thick and a bit sticky. Its smooth avocado flavor works well with lemons, chilies, salsas and strong herbs (cilantro for instance). It has a high smoking point so it can be interchanged with olive oil. It's loaded with antioxidants and vitamins. It helps reduce levels of "bad" (LDL) cholesterol and balances the "good" (HDL) cholesterol levels. I love sautéing with this oil.

Rice Bran Oil: This is one of the newest and latest discoveries in the world of cooking oils. It's clear with a nut like flavor. Its high smoking point makes it great for frying and sautéing. This oil is also loaded with health benefits – a formidable antioxidant. It helps protect against cellular damage and preserves youth. This oil is worth exploring and including in our kitchen repertoire!

Be very careful how you store your oils. They are fragile and go rancid if stored carelessly. They need a cool, dark location. If stored in the refrigerator some may solidify. That's okay; just set them on the counter for an hour before using and they'll return to liquids.

Saturated Fats, Unsaturated Fats and Monosaturated Fats: The general consensus between dietitians, nutritionists and other experts is that saturated fat is less healthful than unsaturated fat. However the overall health impact of saturated fat remains controversial. Some researchers believe it may increase the risk of heart disease while others believe moderate amounts might benefit overall health.

Saturated fats: Are tightly packed with no double bonds between the fatty acids. There are some exceptions but most are solid at room temperature. In fact they contain a high proportion of fatty acid molecules without double bonds and are considered to be less healthy in the diet than unsaturated fat.

Unsaturated Fats: Are loosely packed. They tend to be liquid at room temperature. In fact they contain a high proportion of fatty acid molecules with a least one double bond considered to be healthier in the diet than saturated fat.

Monosaturated Fats: Are healthy fats found in olive oil, avocados and certain nuts. In fact the evidence shows that monounsaturated fats have a number of health benefits. They can help with weight loss, reduce the risk of heart disease and decrease inflammation.

Pasta

For most people cooking pasta is a no brainer. Put it in boiling water and walk away. Not all pasta shapes are created equal and some are better suited to thick sauces while some are perfect for oil based sauces. For delicate sauces spaghetti or other long pasta are a good choice as the thin sauce coats the pasta evenly. For heavier sauces tube pasta such as penne or other large shapes are ideal. The crevices in the pasta trap the hearty sauce and let you get the perfect ratio of sauce to pasta in every bite.

I believe pasta is a noodle designed to capture the sauce, smooth or ribbed or short, to hold it, to transport it in the proper quantity to the mouth and to define the flavor of the recipe. The ribbings increase the surface area to extend the staying power of the sour or sweet notes of the various seasoning. The loops catch small fragments of flavor; the spirals withhold and amplify the density of sauces. Pasta was created as a carrier of sauces and there are no limits to it.

Flour: You can make homemade pasta with many different flours. Experiment! It's half the fun. When it comes to pasta I tend to think of flours on a spectrum of silky and fine to hearty and substantial. The type of flour you use will help dictate the personality and grip of your noodles, but the idea that you need super specific flours to start making wonderful, beautiful, delicious pasta is no good.

Eggs: My basic everyday pasta recipe (the one we're working with today) calls for two eggs. I've made lots of pasta with a higher ratio of eggs, and I sometimes make pasta with no egg. I like two eggs. It lends little richness, color, elasticity and durability to the dough that I find makes the pasta quite versatile. Especially if I'm making a good amount of pasta for freezing later. Meaning I'm not sure what sort of sauce or preparation I'll do. Good quality eggs matter.

Extra-virgin olive oil: I feel like it helps the dough hydrate and helps facilitate smooth rolling through the pasta maker rollers if you're going that route.

Fine-grain sea salt: You want to salt your pasta dough and your pasta water.

Pasta tools

Rolling Pin: If you're starting out and making pasta by hand a rolling pin should do the job. In a pinch if you're short the rolling pin a tall water bottle could do the trick.

Pasta Maker: The Atlas 150 pasta maker is a workhorse. You can collect different attachments over time to experiment with different pasta shapes. With a bit of practice it makes rolling pasta dough to uniform thickness a breeze. You'll need a counter or tabletop to clamp it to. An alternative? A lot of people like to mix their dough in a stand mixer and use the Kitchen Aid Pasta Roller & Cutter attachment to finish their pasta.

Pasta Drying Racks: Let me be honest I don't use any of them. If I want to save pasta for later I freeze it. I did buy a stack of these Eppicotispai drying racks but use them for herbs and chilies more than anything else.

Beautiful Pasta Accessories: I've always had a soft spot for beautiful pasta tools and will soon have an assembled bit of a collection. I'm sure I'll get a bit for Christmas! I read about how to make garganelli pasta on the internet. Some of my favorites are a traditional garganelli board and a new LA Gondola brass tool or pasta stamp. These tools will make them perfectly every time and my fantasy is that I will someday be able to use a Mattarella to roll out a perfect sfoglini pasta. That's where I'm at in my pasta journey.

Spray Bottle & Dough Scraper: I'll put these two items in the bonus category. They're nice to have, but not necessary. I like the spray bottle to control the amount of water in my pasta dough. You don't want your dough to get too wet. The spray bottle allows you to mist it if necessary to add hydration a bit at a time. The dough scraper is great for cleaning flour off countertops, wrangling run-away liquids when they break through flour walls and cutting dough into pieces.

Kitchen decorating

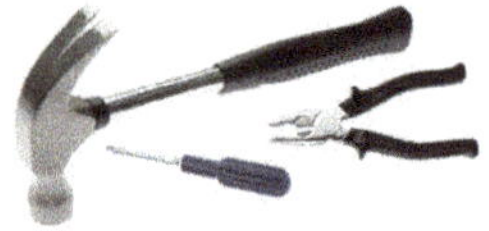

Decorating tips on when to make a kitchen more spacious: If you're not blessed with excess square footage decorating and making your space feel truly livable can be a challenge. The shortage often results in focusing on the practical instead of the pretty which is less than ideal if you're a design lover like me. Read on and get ready to live large.

I have great respect for experts. When it comes to kitchen repair I'll admit I'm not one nor am I very handy. I'm the kind of control freak who has to do everything myself or if it's not done right I love nothing more than calling up a good repairman or contractor who can use their hard-won-knowledge to improve something and make it better than I could ever have imagined. But despite the number of projects that need attention around my house our approach this winter is different.

There also are shortages of labor and materials that force us as homeowners to learn valuable lessons about patience and encourage us to acquire some new skills. Where I would have picked up the phone to hire someone to repair a problem now I'm trying to see if we can do it ourselves.

If you're dreaming of a kitchen renovation before you knock down any walls start small and give the heart of your home a well-deserved upgrade using these stylish upgrades for inspiration. Simple swaps can update your kitchen in a flash.

These ideas span a wide array of different styles and preferences whether you're seeking out a modern, all white kitchen or you're hoping to mix earthy humes to complete your décor ideas. There are designs for any budget no matter if you're penny pinching or splurging on a full renovation. Even if you're just curious for some creative tips these are instant inspiration to any kitchen. With so many kitchen trends you're bound to be itching to incorporate some new kitchen décor ideas into the best room of your house. After all it's the place where your family gathers at least once every day. It's only natural that you want it to look amazing.

These ideas include some kitchen island ideas to improve the spaces focal point or upgrade your hardware for a subtle effect. A kitchen of any size can feel roomy if you know a few tricks. Sticking to white cabinets and walls are a good start but there are many other ways to create extra room in your kitchen or create the illusion of a bigger space than you have all without sacrificing a sense of personality.

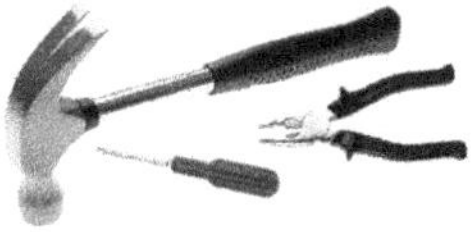

Here are some ways to balance storage, style and long sightliness to get a functional layout with a spacious vibe.

Consider shallow cabinets - Using slimmer, lower cabinets for one area has its advantages. It opens a bit more floor space which can make a big difference in a tight kitchen. It also reduces your storage slightly but often the backs of deep cabinets are hard to reach anyway so the shallower cabinets can be will be just right for everyday items.

Reduce your hardware - Eliminate counter clutter is important for keeping a kitchen looking open and breezy but you can take this a step further by removing the hardware. Using cabinet doors with touch activated latches or integrated reach in pulls reinforces the clean lines of your new kitchen which subtly helps it appear bigger. It also gives you fewer little items to bump into or get caught on your clothing so the space will feel easier to move into.

Rethink the double sink - Large double sinks have their uses but if you're willing to compromise and choose a single sink it can open up better storage options and more unbroken counter space. This applies especially to stock cabinet line which include a limited number of size options. If your sink is centered on the window without a ton of room on either side this can create a dead zone next to it that can't accommodate anything. Using a smaller cabinet for the sink frees up room on either side which can open up new options for adjacent cabinets.

Cook tops and stove top appliances - Not prepared to choose compact appliances? You can still get a much lighter look. Panel ready appliances usually fridges and dishwashers are designed to be able to receive a door front of your choosing so they can blend into the look of your kitchen cabinets. The end look is more fluid which creates an overall larger and airier appearance. It's usually not an inexpensive upgrade but it definitely creates a look of sophisticated luxury.

Add glass door cabinets - Here's another way to lighten up your uppers but without actually changing your storage. Switch out typical solid cabinet fronts to doors with glass inserts to make the look much airier. Use this cabinet to display attractive drinkware or use frosted glass so you only get a faint peek at the mishmash of items stored within.

Use a Short Backsplash - To make the wall look 10 feet tall try using a short minimal backsplash in a color that blends with the wall. The lack of an obvious dividing line between where the tile stops and the plain wall starts keep the planes of the wall looking taller so your open space looks positively vast. Try a backsplash to present a subtle sheen that almost acts

like a mirror giving the room a sense of depth and echoing the finishes of steel appliances or fixture.

Stash and hide - Because you can never have too much storage, stash bulky appliances, like stand mixers behind a sliding cabinet door. Or for a faster solution, turn to good old baskets to hold and conceal seasonal goods like holiday cookie cutters or sprinklers.

Stacking shelving - Replace your cabinets with floating shelves to make your kitchen feel bigger and brighter.

Moody hues - Black adds a hint of posh style to any cooking space. For a less stark but equally chic option "almost black" colors that are rich and ware like deep blues and cozy maroons.

Juxtapose material - Incorporate multiple kinds of natural stone, different shades of wood, and both matte and glossy surface for a custom look that's not too matchy.

Finishing touches - Update your hardware or showing off items you have hidden in cabinets to update your existing kitchen in a single afternoon.

Colorful lighting - Think of lighting as jewelry for your kitchen - the right kind can tie the whole room together or stand out to make a statement.

Eye-catching tile - Have fun! A playful pattern adds major wow factor to a backsplash or statement floor.

Painted floors - Of all the kitchen paint trends this is a favorite. Grab some painter's tape plus some pretty colors and say goodbye to boring floor forever.

Upper storage - Floating shelves may be all the rage but make the case for mixing both open shelves and traditional upper cabinets. Try placing shelves around a kitchen window to allow more light to filter in.

Moveable addition - Want a bigger island without having to renovate. You can double your island in one fell swoop by placing a light dining table right up next to it.

Bright and airy - Some kitchens embrace the light with crisp white cabinetry and a soft blue tile backsplash to compliment the room's sunny view.

Mixed styles - House flipping pros have the winning kitchen design formula down to a science by incorporating both modern and traditional elements.

Painted ceilings - Paint is the quickest and most effective way to transform your kitchen. Taken it to the next level by covering the ceiling. Just to be sure to keep a few pieces of wall white to strike and even balance of color.

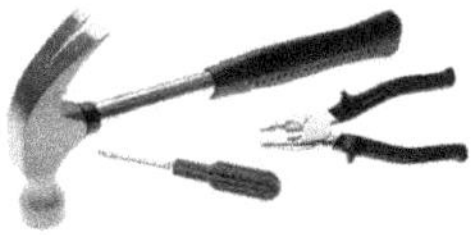

Classic aesthetic - When in doubt opt for classics like bistro chairs and subway tile that always stands the test of time. Pretty hydrangeas on the counter don't hurt either.

Double duty table - Let a rustic dining table double as a comfy prep station for big family meals this summer.

Durable countertops - Scratch-resistant is best for easy cleaning. A striped rug adds comfort underfoot.

Island storage - Hide linens, platters and single use items under the island. Hidden cabinets on both sides double up as a place to stash pots and pans.

Instant dinner table - Extend the countertop over the edge of a black island and it transforms into a casual dining spot. Chick shades let you filter in just the right amount of lighting.

PASTA

SHRIMP FETTUCINE ALFREDO

Serving size = 4; cook time = 20 minutes

Ingredients

1 (9 oz) pkg refrigerated fettuccine
1 lb peeled and deveined medium shrimp
2 green onions, chopped
2 garlic cloves, minced
2 tsp olive oil
½ cup grated parmesan-reggiano cheese
1/3 cup half and half
3 tbsp 1/3-less fat cream cheese
¼ tsp freshly ground black pepper
2 tbsp chopped fresh parsley

Directions

Boil pasta for about 10 minutes. Reserve ¼ cup pasta water. Drain pasta and rinse with hot water. Combine shrimp, onions and garlic in a small bowl. Heat a large skillet over medium high heat. Add olive oil and swirl to coat. Add shrimp mixture and sauté for 4 minutes or until shrimp are done. Remove from pan; keep warm. Reduce heat to medium. Add reserved cooking liquid, parmigiana-reggiano, half and half, cream cheese and pepper to pan. Cook for 2 minutes or until cheeses melt. Combine pasta, cheese mixture and shrimp mixture. Sprinkle with parsley.

CACIO PEPE

Serving size = 2-3; cook time = 15 minutes

"A definite family favorite. You don't even have to tweak it to make it better."

Ingredients

½ lb pasta, any kind
2 tbsp butter, divided
1 tbsp extra virgin olive oil
Coarsely ground black pepper
¾ cup freshly grated pecorino,
plus more for garnish
¾ cup freshly grated parmesan,
plus more for garnish

Directions

Boil pasta for about 10 minutes. Reserve 2/3 cup pasta water. Drain noodles and rinse with hot water. In a large skillet over medium heat, melt 1 tablespoon butter with oil. Add a generous amount of black pepper and toast until fragrant about 1 minute. Add ½ cup reserved pasta water and bring to a simmer. Whisk in remaining butter. Using tongs toss pasta into butter mixture. Add cheeses and toss constantly until cheeses are melty removing skillet from heat when about half the cheese has melted. If sauce is too thick loosen with more pasta water.

SHRIMP LOUIE PASTA

Serving size = 3; cook time = 55 minutes

Ingredients
3 cups rotini, uncooked
1 cup mayonnaise
½ cup ranch dressing
1/3 cup seafood cocktail sauce
2 tablespoons fresh lemon juice
1 teaspoon Worcestershire sauce
Salt and Pepper
1 lb medium cooked shrimp,
peeled & deveined
½ cup chopped fresh tomato
½ cup sliced green onion
½ cup chopped sweet red pepper
2 tablespoons chopped fresh parsley

Directions
Boil pasta for about 10 minutes. Drain noodles and rinse with cold water. Meanwhile in a large bowl whisk together mayonnaise, ranch dressing, seafood cocktail sauce, lemon juice, Worcestershire sauce and salt and pepper. Stir in cooled pasta and remaining ingredients. Serve immediately or cover and refrigerate.

PASTA PUTTANESCA

Serving size = 3-6; cook time = 30 minutes

Ingredients

1 lb linguine or other long pasta
3 tbsp olive oil
3 or more cloves garlic, lightly
smashed and peeled
3 or more anchovy fillets
1 (28 oz) can whole plum tomatoes
Freshly ground black pepper to taste
½ cup pitted black olives, preferably oil cured
2 tbsp capers
Crushed red pepper flakes to taste
Chopped fresh parsley, oregano, marjoram
or basil leaves for garnish, optional
Salt to taste

Directions

Warm 2 tablespoons oil with garlic and anchovies in skillet over medium low heat. Cook stirring occasionally until garlic is lightly golden. Drain tomatoes and crush with fork or hands. Add to skillet with some salt and pepper. Raise heat to medium high and cook stirring occasionally until tomatoes break down and mixture becomes saucy about 10 minutes. Sir in olives, capers and red pepper flakes and continue to simmer. Boil pasta for about 10 minutes. Drain noodles and rinse with hot water. Add pasta to sauce and remaining tablespoon of oil. Combine well. Taste and adjust seasonings as necessary. Garnish with herbs if you like and serve.

quickly stir in pasta and egg mixture and gently toss to combine. Season with salt and pepper to taste. Add reserved pasta water one tablespoon at a time until desired consistency is reached. Serve immediately garnished with parsley if desired.

PASTA CARBONARA

Serving size = 4; cook time = 30 minutes

Ingredients

8 oz spaghetti
2 lrg eggs
½ cup freshly grated parmesan
4 slices bacon, diced
4 cloves garlic, minced
Kosher salt and freshly ground
black pepper to taste
2 tbsp chopped fresh parsley leaves

Directions

Boil pasta for about 10 minutes. Reserve ½ cup water. Drain noodles and rinse with hot water. In a small bowl whisk together eggs and parmesan; set aside. Heat a large skillet over medium high heat. Add bacon and cook until brown and crispy about 6 to 8 minutes and reserve excess fat. Stir in garlic until fragrant about 1 minute. Reduce heat to low. Working

SPAGHETTI AND MEATBALLS

Serving size = 4-5; cook time = 1 ½ hour

Ingredients

2 tbsp extra virgin olive oil
½ chopped sweet yellow onion
3 cloves chopped garlic
1 cup very finely chopped carrots
1 cup chopped cremini brown mushrooms
2 (28 oz) cans italian plum tomatoes
¼ cup chopped fresh italian parsley
¼ cup chopped fresh basil
3 tbsp tomato paste
¼ cup grated parmesan-
romano cheese blend
Salt to taste about 1 tsp
¼ cup red wine
For the meatballs
1 lb ground beef at least 16% fat
½ lb fresh bulk italian style pork sausage
2 tbsp finely chopped basil
2 tbsp finely chopped italian parsley
½ cup finely chopped cremini
brown mushrooms
2 lrg eggs
¾ cup unseasoned breadcrumbs
¼ cup grated parmesan
romano cheese blend
2 tsp sea salt
2 tsp fresh ground black pepper
1 tbsp extra virgin olive oil
Red wine
Water

For the pasta

1 ½ lb spaghetti, thin spaghetti or bucatini

Directions

Prepare the sauce: Heat olive oil in a 4 to 5 qt pot on medium high heat. Add onions and cook for 2 minutes, garlic and cook for 30 seconds longer or until fragrant. Carrots and mushrooms cook for 2 minutes. Add the tomato paste concentrate. Stir to blend and cook for a minute longer. Add the canned tomatoes, basil and parsley. Mash and stir the tomatoes with a potato masher until the sauce starts to thicken about 5 minutes over medium high heat. Reduce heat to low and simmer gently while preparing meatballs, stirring occasionally. Add water if needed.

Form the meatballs: In a large bowl mix by hand the beef, Italian sausage, basil, parsley, mushrooms, eggs, breadcrumbs, cheese, salt and pepper. Do not over mix or the meatballs will be tough. Use a small melon baller or a teaspoon to form 1 inch round meatballs. Roll and compress into tight balls.

Brown the meatballs: In a separate wide shallow pan heat the olive oil on medium high heat. Brown meatballs on all sides about 2 to 3 minutes. Depending on pan size you may need to brown two batches of the meatballs. Cook them in a single layer and do not crowd the pan by stacking them. Do not overcook the meatballs. They will continue to cook in the sauce. You just want to brown them on all sides. Towards the end of browning the meatballs add a little bit of red wine to deglaze the pan.

Finish and simmer the sauce: Add the red wine to the sauce and stir in the cheese. Add salt to taste. Add meatballs and gently stir. Simmer the sauce and meatballs for 30 to 45 minutes stirring occasionally.

Cook the spaghetti: Boil pasta for about 10 minutes. Drain noodles and rinse with hot water. *Serve*: To serve place a thin layer of sauce on plate, add pasta, add sauce and meatballs and then sprinkle with grated parmesan romano cheese.

BAKED MOSTACCIOLI

Serving size = 4; cook time = 1 hour

Ingredients

8 oz uncooked mostaccioli
1 ½ lb ground beef
½ cup chopped onion
1 garlic clove minced
1 can (28 oz) diced tomatoes
1 can (8 oz) tomato sauce
1 can (6 oz) tomato paste
1 can (4 oz) sliced mushrooms
½ cup water
1 - 1 ¼ tsp salt
1 tsp sugar
1 tsp dried basil
1/8 tsp pepper
1 bay leaf
2 c shredded part skim mozzarella cheese
½ c grated parmesan cheese

Directions

Preheat oven to 350 degrees. Boil pasta for about 10 minutes. Drain noodles and rinse with hot water. Set aside. Meanwhile in a large saucepan cook beef and onion over medium heat until meat is no longer pink. Add garlic and cook 1 minute. Drain. Stir in tomatoes, tomato sauce and paste, mushrooms, water, salt, sugar, basil, pepper and bay leaf. Bring to a boil. Reduce heat; simmer, uncovered 30 minutes stirring occasionally. Discard bay leaf. Stir in mostaccioli. Spoon into a 13x9 inch baking dish. Sprinkle with parmesan cheese. Cover and bake for 1 hour or until bubbly. Let stand 5 minutes before serving.

FETTUCCINI ALFREDO

Serving size = 4; cook time = 30 minutes

Ingredients

12 oz cauliflower florets (1 small cauliflower)
½ cup grated parmesan cheese,
  more for serving
¼ cup extra virgin olive oil
2 garlic cloves
½ tsp Dijon mustard
3 tbsp unsalted butter
2 tbsp fresh lemon juice
1 tsp sea salt
Freshly ground black pepper
16 oz fettucine pasta
1 to 1 ½ cups reserved pasta cooking water
Chopped fresh parsley

Directions

Bring a large pot of salted water to a boil. Add the cauliflower and boil until the cauliflower is fork tender 8 to 10 minutes. Drain and place the cauliflower in a blender. Add the parmesan cheese, olive oil, garlic, mustard, butter, lemon juice, salt and several grinds of pepper. Boil pasta for about 10 minutes. Reserve 1½ cups of pasta water. Drain noodles and rinse with hot water. Add 1 cup of the pasta water to the blender and blend the sauce until creamy. Transfer the pasta to a large bowl or skillet. Add the sauce and toss to coat. If you prefer a looser sauce add the remaining ½ cup pasta water and toss again. Sprinkle with parsley and season to taste. Serve with grated cheese on the side.

PENNE ALLA VODKA

Serving size = 6; cook time = 30 minutes

Ingredients

1 (28 oz) can San Marzano tomatoes crushed finely with hands
2 tbsp extra virgin olive oil
½ cup minced yellow onion
3 oz prosciutto, diced (optional)
1 tbsp minced garlic (3 cloves)
Salt and freshly ground black pepper
½ cup vodka
¼ tsp red pepper flakes more or less to taste
2/3 cup heavy cream
¼ cup finely shredded parmesan cheese, plus more for serving
1 tbsp chopped fresh oregano
¼ cup chopped fresh basil
14 oz penne pasta, plus reserved pasta water for thinning sauce as needed

Directions

Heat oil in a large pot over medium heat. Add onion and prosciutto. Sauté 4 to 5 minutes, add garlic and red pepper flakes and sauté 1 minute longer. Remove pan from heat and add tomatoes, vodka, season with salt and pepper to taste. Return to medium high heat and bring to a simmer. Reduce heat to medium low and let simmer until strong alcohol scent has cooked off, about 15 minutes stirring occasionally.

Meanwhile boil pasta for about 10 minutes. Reserve 1½ cup pasta water. Drain noodles and rinse with hot water. Stir cream into sauce and let just heat through about 1 minute. Stir in parmesan, basil and oregano. Add drained pasta to pot with sauce. Toss to coat while thinning sauce with a little pasta water as needed. Serve warm with more parmesan and garnish with more basil if desired.

GOULASH

Serving size = 6; cook time = 30 minutes

Ingredients

2 tbsp extra virgin olive oil
1 medium yellow onion, chopped
2 cloves garlic, minced
1 lb ground beef
Kosher salt
Freshly ground black pepper
1 tbsp tomato paste
1 ¼ cup low sodium beef broth
1 (15 oz) can tomato sauce
1 (15 oz) can diced tomatoes
1 tsp Italian seasoning
1 tsp paprika
1 ½ cup elbow macaroni, uncooked
1 cup shredded cheddar
Freshly chopped parsley, for garnish

Directions

Boil pasta for about 10 minutes. Drain noodles and rinse with hot water. Set aside. In a large skillet over medium heat, heat oil. Add onion and cook until soft about 5 minutes. Add garlic and cook until fragrant about 1 minute more. Add ground beef and cook until no longer pink, about 6 minutes. Drain fat and return to pan. Season with salt and pepper. Add tomato paste and stir to coat then pour in broth, tomato sauce and diced tomatoes. Season with Italian seasoning and paprika and stir in macaroni. Bring to a simmer and cook, stirring occasionally. Stir in cheese and remove from heat. Garnish with parsley before serving.

CREAMY FETTUCCINE ALFREDO

Serving size = 4; cook time = 30 minutes

Ingredients
Kosher salt
1 lb fettuccine
½ cup heavy cream
½ cup butter
½ cup freshly grated Parmesan,
plus more for sprinkling
Freshly ground black pepper
2 tbsp chopped parsley

Directions
Boil pasta for about 10 minutes. Reserve about 1 cup of pasta water. Drain noodles and rinse with hot water. Meanwhile in a large skillet over medium heat add cream and butter. Cook until the butter is melted and the cream is heated through. Whisk in Parmesan and season with salt and pepper. Add cooked pasta and toss until coated in sauce. If the sauce is too thick add reserved pasta water 1 tablespoon at a time. Garnish with parsley and serve immediately.

CAPRESE CHICKEN PASTA

Serving size = 4; cook time = 30 minutes

Ingredients

1 lb boneless skinless chicken breasts

Balsamic Chicken Marinade

¼ cup olive oil
3 tbsp balsamic vinegar
1 tbsp Dijon mustard
1 tbsp lemon juice
2 tsp brown sugar
1 tsp each dried basil, garlic powder, onion powder
½ tsp salt
¼ tsp pepper

Roasted Vegetables

1-12 oz pkg cherry tomatoes
1 sm zucchini, halved and sliced
½ bunch asparagus, ends trimmed, cut into 1″ pieces
4-6 garlic cloves, minced
1 tbsp olive oil
2 tbsp reserved marinade – (in directions)
½ tsp salt
¼ tsp pepper

Pasta

1 lb linguine or thin spaghetti
1 c reserved pasta water
1 tbsp lemon juice
1 tbsp balsamic vinegar
¼ c loosely packed fresh parsley, chopped
¼ c loosely packed fresh basil, chopped
1 c freshly Parmesan cheese, more or less
1 c mozzarella snacking balls or pearls, more or less

Directions

MARINADE: Whisk together all of the Balsamic Marinade ingredients in a medium bowl. Remove 2 tablespoons to a large bowl along with tomatoes, asparagus, zucchini, 1 tablespoon olive oil, ½ tsp salt and ¼ tsp pepper. Toss evenly to coat. Refrigerate. Add remaining marinade to a large ziploc bag along with chicken. Marinate 2-8 hours.

CHICKEN: When ready to cook let chicken sit at room temperature for 15 to 30 minutes. Heat a large non-stick skillet over medium high heat. Once very hot add chicken and cook undisturbed for 3 to 5 minutes or until nicely browned (or blackened if you prefer) on one side. Turn chicken over cover and reduce heat to medium. Cook for approximately 5 to 7 more minutes (depending on thickness of chicken) or until chicken is cooked through. Remove to a cutting board and let rest 5 minutes before slicing.

ROASTED VEGETABLES: Meanwhile, preheat oven to 400 degrees. Add vegetables, garlic, olive oil, reserved marinade, salt and pepper to baking sheet and toss to combine. Line vegetables on a baking sheet in a single layer. Roast for 12 to 15 minutes or until asparagus is crisp tender.

PASTA: Meanwhile, boil pasta for about 10 minutes. Reserve 1 cup pasta water. Drain noodles and rinse with hot water. Place in a very large mixing bowl or pot.

ASSEMBLE: Add roasted vegetables and all of the oil/juices/seasonings from the baking sheet to the pasta, along with 1 tablespoon lemon juice, 1 tablespoon balsamic vinegar, fresh parsley and fresh basil. Add reserved pasta water (a little at a time, I used ½ cup) to reach desired consistency. Ad desired amount of Parmesan and mozzarella pearls. Taste and add additional salt and pepper, and red pepper if desired.

Optional: Garnish with additional freshly grated Parmesan.

GARLICKY SPAGHETTI WITH GREENS

Serving size = 6; cook time = 1 hour

Ingredients

¾ c extra-virgin olive oil
1 c panko
2 tbsp finely chopped parsley
Kosher salt
Pepper
1 lb spaghetti
2/3 c thinly sliced garlic (about 18 cloves)
2 lbs mustard greens and kale, stemmed and leaves coarsely torn
2 tbsp fresh lemon juice

Directions

In a small skillet heat ¼ cup of the olive oil. Add the panko and toast over moderate heat stirring until golden about 15 minutes. Meanwhile boil pasta for about 10 minutes. Reserve 1 cup of the pasta water. Drain noodles and rinse with hot water. In a large pot combine the remaining ½ cup of oil with the garlic and cook over low heat stirring occasionally until the garlic is fragrant and light golden 7 to 8 minutes.

In batches add the greens and cook tossing until wilted about 3 minutes. Season with salt and pepper. Add the pasta, ½ cup of the reserved pasta water and the lemon juice; cook, stirring until a sauce forms for 2 minutes. Divide the pasta among bowls and top with the panko.

SPINACH LASAGNA

Serving size = 8; cook time = 1 hour 15 minutes

Ingredients

12 to 16 dried or fresh lasagna noodles
3 to 4 c good tomato sauce
2 tbsp extra virgin olive oil
3 c cooked spinach squeezed dry and chopped (about 1 ½ lb fresh)
1 ½ cups ricotta
1 ½ c coarsely grated mozzarella
2 c grated parmesan
Salt and freshly ground black pepper

Directions

If you are using dried pasta boil pasta for about 10-12 minutes. If you are using fresh pasta sheets cut them into long wide noodles approximately 3 inches by 13 inches or a size that will fit into your lasagna dish. Drain and then lay the noodles flat on a towel so they won't stick.

Heat oven to 400 degrees. Grease a rectangular baking dish with the olive oil, add a large dollop of tomato sauce and spread it around. Put a layer of noodles in the dish trimming any overhanging edges. Top with a layer of tomato sauce, one third of the spinach and one fourth of the ricotta (use your fingers to spread it evenly) the mozzarella and the Parmesan. Season with salt and pepper if desired.

Repeat the layers twice and top with the remaining noodles, tomato sauce, ricotta, mozzarella and Parmesan; the top should be covered with cheese; and more ricotta and parmesan as needed. (The lasagna may be made ahead to this point, wrapped tightly and refrigerated for up to a day or frozen. Bring to room temperature before proceeding.)

Bake until the lasagna is bubbling and the cheese is melted and lightly browned on top about 45 minutes. Remove from the oven and let rest a few minutes before serving or cool completely. Cover well and refrigerate for up to 4 days, or freeze.

CHICKEN TETRAZZINI

Serving size = 6-8; cook time = 50 minutes

Ingredients
For the tetrazzini
12 oz thin spaghetti or linguine
4 c shredded rotisserie chicken or
 cook 2 lb chicken breast.
1 lb button mushrooms thickly sliced
1 medium onion finely hopped
3 to 4 garlic cloves minced
2 tbsp olive oil

For the creamy sauce:
4 tbsp unsalted butter
1/3 c all-purpose flour
2 ½ c low sodium chicken broth
1 tbsp lemon juice
1 ½ c half and half or sub with equal parts milk and heavy ream
1 tsp sea salt or to taste
¼ tsp black pepper freshly ground
½ c parsley chopped plus more to garnish
1 ½ c shredded mozzarella cheese

Directions
Preheat oven to 350 F. Boil pasta for about 10 minutes. Drain noodles and rinse with hot water. Set aside. Cut 4 cups of chicken meat from a rotisserie chicken and shred into bite sized pieces and set aside. Place a large dutch oven or pot over medium high heat. Add 2 tbsp oil then add sliced mushrooms and sauté 3 minutes or until softened. Add diced onions and cook until onions are soft and golden 5 to 7 minutes.

Add minced garlic and sauté another 1 to 2 min until fragrant. Remove to the cutting board with chicken. In the same pot melt 4 tbsp butter and whisk in 1/3 cup flour until lightly golden (1 ½ min). Add 2 ½ cups chicken broth, 1 tbsp lemon juice, 1 tsp salt, ¼ tsp pepper and whisk until smooth. Add 1 ½ cups half and half and bring to a simmer. Season sauce with more salt and pepper to taste.

Return chicken, mushrooms, onions and pasta to the pot then sprinkle in ¼ cup chopped fresh parsley and stir to combine. Sprinkle the top generously with shredded mozzarella. Cover and bake at 350 degrees F for 30 minutes then remove lid and continue baking 15 minutes.

Recipe Notes: To cook your own chicken in your dutch oven or pot melt 1 tbsp butter and 1 tbsp oil over medium high heat. Season 2 lb chicken breasts with about ½ tsp salt and ¼ tsp pepper. Once oil is hot sauté chicken until golden brown on both sides and cooked through (about 4 min per side). Remove to cutting board to cool then cut into bite sized pieces. If baking in a 13 x 9 inch casserole dish cover with foil and bake 25 to 30 minutes then bake uncovered an additional 10 to 15 min (it bakes 5 to 10 minutes faster in a casserole dish.)

PASTA WITH SAUSAGE, OLIVES, SUN DRIED TOMATOES AND CREAM

Serving size = 6; cook time = 30 minutes

Ingredients

2 tbsp extra virgin olive oil
1 med yellow onion, finely diced
1 med clove garlic, finely chopped
1 - ¼ lb hot italian sausage, casings removed
½ c dry white wine (can be the same
    wine as for the mussels, above)
1 c pitted Kalamata olives, coarsely chopped
1 c oil packed sun dried tomato halves
    drained and coarsely chopped
1 c heavy cream
¼ c chopped fresh flat leaf parsley
¼ c grated parmigiana-reggiano
1 lb dried rotini
Kosher salt and freshly ground black pepper

Directions

In a large sauté pan heat the olive oil over medium heat. Add the onion and cook until softened about 5 minutes. Add the garlic and cook for 1 minute. Add the sausage and cook breaking it into bite size pieces with a spoon until just cooked through 6 to 8 minutes. Spoon off the fat if it's excessive.

Add the wine, increase the heat to medium high and cook scraping up any browned bits in the pan until most of the wine is evaporated about 3 to 5 minutes. Stir in the olives and sun dried tomatoes and cook for 2 minutes. Add the cream and increase the heat to high, bring to a boil and cook stirring occasionally until the cream thickens slightly 2 to 5 minutes. Stir in about 2 tablespoons of the parsley and 2 tablespoons of the parmigiana. Keep the sauce warm over low heat.

Boil pasta for about 10 minutes. Reserve ¼ cup of the pasta water. Drain noodles and rinse with hot water. Set aside. Return the pasta to its pot. Add the sauce and the reserved cooking water and set the pot over high heat. Gently toss the pasta for 30 to 60 seconds and season to taste with salt and pepper. Divide among warm bowls and sprinkle with the remaining 2 tablespoons parmigiana and 2 tablespoons parsley.

TUSCAN MAC AND CHEESE

Serving size = 6; cook time = 30 minutes

Ingredients

9 oz jarred sun dried tomato strips in oil (reserve 2 tablespoons of oil and drain the rest)
6 cloves garlic finely diced
3 c milk or light cream or half and half divided
3 c baby spinach leaves
2 large skinless boneless chicken breasts pounded to 1 inch thickness (or 4 boneless and skinless chicken thigh fillets)
Salt and pepper to season
½ tsp paprika (sweet and smoky)
3 level tbsp flour
10 oz elbow macaroni uncooked (3 cups)
2 tsp dried italian herbs
2 tbsp fresh parsley chopped
2 c chicken broth
2 tbsp butter
1 tbsp oil, divided (use olive oil or canola)
1 sm yellow onion chopped
1 c fresh grated parmesan cheese
½ tsp dried parsley
½ c grated cheese cheddar or gruyere
1/3 c white wine OPTIONAL (use chicken broth instead if you wish)
¾ c mozzarella cheese shredded

Directions

Season chicken with salt, pepper, paprika, dried parsley and 2 teaspoons of the oil. Heat the remaining oil in a large pot or pan over medium high heat. Add the chicken and sear on both sides until golden brown, cooked through and no longer pink in the middle. Transfer chicken to a warm plate, tent with foil and set aside. Fry the garlic and onion with butter until the onions becomes transparent in the same pan.

Pour in the white wine and allow to simmer for 5 minutes or until beginning to reduce down. Add the sun dried tomatoes with 2 tablespoons of the sun dried tomato oil from the jar and cook for 1 to 2 minutes. Stir the flour into the pot and allow to cook for a further minute. Then add the broth, 2 ½ cups of milks, herbs, salt and pepper and bring to a very low simmer.

Add the dry macaroni and stir occasionally as it comes to a simmer. Reduce heat down to medium low and stir regularly while it cooks for about 9 to 10 minutes or until the sauce thickens and the macaroni is just cooked. Add the spinach and stir through until wilted. Take the pot off the stove and stir all of the cheese in quickly. Adjust salt and pepper to taste. If the sauce is too thick add the remaining ½ cup milk or cream in ¼ cup increments until reaching desired thickness.

The sauce will continue to thicken as it cools. Slice the chicken into strips and stir through the pasta and pour in juices left from the chicken. Sprinkle with parsley and stir through. Everything is ready to serve on your dining table.

Recipe notes: Full fat milk is preferred for maximum flavor but low fat milk is ok. You can also use a light cream, heavy cream or evaporated milk. For added cream flavor add in ½ cup light cream or heavy cream if you wish right before adding in the spinach. Allow it to get hot before adding in the spinach!

SHRIMP BOIL PASTA

Serving size = 4; cook time = 30 minutes

Ingredients

2 tbsp old bay seasoning
1 lb spaghetti
1 tbsp extra virgin olive oil
1 med onion chopped
1 lb andouille or kielbasa sliced
into coins size pieces
2 c fresh corn cut from the cobb
1 lb med shrimp peeled and deveined
4 green onions thinly sliced

Directions

Add 2 tablespoons Old Bay to a large pot of salted boiling water. Boil pasta for about 10 minutes. Reserve 1 cup pasta water. Drain noodles and rinse with hot water. Meanwhile heat olive oil in a large skillet over medium heat. Add onion, cook until tender about 5 minutes. Stir in sausage until heated through and begins to brown. Add corn, shrimp, and reserved pasta water and bring to a simmer. Add cooked spaghetti and green onions; toss until combined.

CAULIFLOWER & BROCCOLI ROTINI CARBONARA

Serving size = 6; cook time = 30 minutes

Ingredients

8 c broccoli florets (see notes)
¼ c (4 tablespoons) extra virgin olive oil, divided
1 ¾ teaspoons kosher salt, divided
¼ teaspoon black pepper, divided
8 c cauliflower florets (see note)
12 oz whole wheat rotini pasta
1 c reserved pasta cooking water
1 c shredded parmesan cheese (see note)
3 tablespoons lemon juice
1 tablespoon minced garlic

Directions

Preheat oven to 475 degrees. On a parchment lined baking sheet toss the broccoli florets with 2 tablespoon olive oil, ¾ teaspoon salt and 1/8 teaspoon pepper, making sure the oil and seasonings are evenly distributed. (If you prefer you can toss the ingredients together in a bowl and then dump the broccoli mixture out onto the baking sheet).

On a second parchment lined baking sheet repeat the process with the cauliflower florets tossing them with 2 tablespoons olive oil, ¾ teaspoons salt and 1/8 teaspoon pepper. Make sure the vegetables are spread out evenly on the baking sheets and not heaped on top of each other so they roast properly rather than steaming.

Place cauliflower in the oven and roast for 5 minutes; then add broccoli to the oven. Roast for 5 minutes more and then stir both cauliflower and broccoli and rotate sheet pans to promote even roasting. Continue roasting for about 10 more minutes (20 minutes total for cauliflower and 15 minutes total for broccoli) until the vegetables have developed some gorgeous roasted brown spots. Remove from oven and set briefly aside keeping warm.

Boil pasta for about 10 minutes. Reserve 1 cup of pasta water. Drain noodles and rinse with hot water. In a large serving bowl, toss the roasted vegetables with the cooked pasta. Sprinkle the parmesan, lemon juice, garlic and remaining ¼ teaspoon salt evenly distributed throughout the pasta and not concentrated in one spot.

Loosen as desired with reserved pasta cooking water (we usually use about ½ - ¾ cup). Taste and adjust the pasta water, lemon juice, and salt as needed. Serve immediately.

PASTA WITH PANCETTA, SHALLOTS AND SAGE

Serving size = 6; cooking time = 1 hour

Ingredients

¼ c extra virgin olive oil
½ lb thinly sliced pancetta
6 large shallots, thinly sliced (2 cups)
¼ c sage leaves, torn
3 plum tomatoes-peeled, seeded
  and cut into ¼ - inch strips
1 lb rigatoni
Salt and freshly ground black pepper
Chile pepper, optional

Directions

In a large skillet heat 1 tablespoon of the olive oil. Add the pancetta and cook over moderately low heat until most of the fat has rendered and the pancetta is golden about 10 minutes. Add the wine and simmer over moderately high heat until evaporated about 3 minutes. With a slotted spoon transfer the pancetta to a bowl. Pour the fat off and return the skillet to the stove.

Heat the remaining 3 tablespoons of olive oil in the skillet. Add the shallots and sage leaves and cook over low heat, stirring occasionally until the shallots are translucent about 8 minutes. Stir in the tomatoes and cook until softened about 4 minutes. Add the pancetta and chile and cook over low heat stirring occasionally until the sauce thickens about 10 minutes.

Boil pasta for about 10 minutes. Reserve ½ cup pasta water. Drain noodles and rinse with hot water. Return the pasta to the pot. Stir in the shallot and pancetta mixture along with the reserved pasta cooking water. Season with salt and pepper toss well and serve.

RAW ZUCCHINI AND SQUASH SPAGHETTI WITH ROASTED CHERRY TOMATOES AND PISTACHIO PESTO

Serving size = 6-8 (if using as a side dish); cooking time = 30 minutes

Ingredients

1 zucchini
1 summer squash
3 c cherry tomatoes
1 ½ c loosely packed basil leaves
1 c loosely packed flat leaf parsley leaves
1 clove garlic
¼ c roasted pistachios
½ c extra virgin olive oil plus more for drizzling cherry tomatoes
Kosher salt
Freshly ground pepper

Directions

Using a spiralizer, create your spaghetti strands from the zucchini and summer squash. Alternatively lay a box grater on its side with the biggest holes facing up. Move your zucchini and summer squash lengthwise across the box grater to create long ribbons.

Preheat oven to 400 degrees F. On a foil lined baking sheet drizzle cherry tomatoes with a little olive oil and toss to coat. Sprinkle with Kosher salt and freshly ground black pepper. Roast for about 10 to 15 minutes until the tomatoes have wrinkled and collapsed slightly.

In a food processor combine the basil parsley, garlic and roasted pistachios until coarsely chopped. Drizzle in olive oil and process until fully combined. Season with Kosher salt and freshly ground pepper. If the pesto is too thick add a little more olive oil until the desired consistency is reached.

In a bowl combine the zucchini spaghetti, roasted tomatoes and any juice that may have spilled out onto the baking sheet during the roasting process and pistachio pesto. Garnish with extra chopped pistachio and basil if desired.

TOMATO RAVIOLI

Serving size = 4 (about 6 ravioli and ½ cup tomato mixture); cooking time = 40 minutes

Ingredients

1 lb cherry tomatoes
2 shallots, cut into wedges
Cooking spray
3 tbsp extra-virgin olive oil, divided
2 tbsp balsamic vinegar
¼ tsp kosher salt
¼ tsp black pepper
12 oz cheese ravioli
2 tbsp chopped fresh basil

Directions

Preheat oven to 425 degrees. Halve half of tomatoes. Arrange cut tomatoes and shallots on a jelly roll pan coated with cooking spray. Drizzle with 1 tablespoon oil; toss. Bake at 425 degrees for 35 minutes. Add 2 tablespoons oil, vinegar, salt, and pepper to pan. Bake 10 minutes. Cook ravioli according to package directions, omitting salt and fat. Drain ravioli reserving ¼ cup cooking liquid. Add ravioli to tomatoes; toss. Add cooking liquid if needed. Garnish with chopped basil.

ROASTED BROCCOLI, SUN DRIED TOMATOES AND MOZZARELLA WITH PASTA

Serving size = 4; cook time = 30 minutes

Ingredients

Kosher salt
12 oz broccoli florets, cut into bite size pieces (about 6 cups)
12 oz rigatoni or other medium pasta
4 oz canned pitted black olives, cut in half lengthwise (about 1 cup)
2 oz sun-dried tomatoes (not oil packed) thinly sliced (about 2/3 cup)
½ oz finely grated Parmigiana-Reggiano (about 1/3 cup); more as needed
½ tsp granulated garlic; more to taste
½ tsp crushed red pepper flakes; more to taste
6 tbsp extra virgin olive oil; more as needed

Directions

Bring a large pot of well salted water to a boil. Add the broccoli and cook until crisp tender 2 to 3 minutes. Using a slotted spoon, transfer the broccoli to a colander; rinse under cold water. Boil pasta for about 10 minutes. Reserve ¼ cup of pasta water. Drain the pasta over the broccoli in the colander, and transfer to a large bowl. Add the olives, tomatoes, cheese, garlic, pepper flakes and ½ tsp salt. Add the olive oil and toss well. Add the reserved cooking water 1 or 2 tablespoons at a time to loosen the pasta. Season to taste with salt, granulated garlic, and pepper flakes. Serve drizzled with additional olive oil and cheese if you like.

CHEESY SHELLS WITH SPINACH AND MUSHROOMS

Serving size = 5; cook time = 30 minutes

Ingredients

8 oz pasta shells (or any pasta of your liking)
2 tbsp olive oil
1 small white onion, diced
1 (8 oz) package mushrooms, sliced
1 cup milk
2 tbsp cornstarch
¼ c shredded parmesan cheese
½ tsp dry mustard
½ tsp salt
¼ tsp pepper
1 c fresh mozzarella, cut into small cubes
12 oz package of baby spinach

Directions

Boil pasta for about 10 minutes. Drain noodles and rinse with hot water. Meanwhile heat olive oil over medium heat in a large skillet. Add onion and cook until translucent about 5 minutes. Add garlic and cook 1 minute. Add mushrooms and sauté until they start to release their liquid. In small bowl, combine milk and cornstarch and stir to combine. Add to onion and mushroom mixture along with parmesan cheese and cook about 2 to 3 minutes stirring constantly.

Add dry mustard, salt, pepper and stir to combine. Add pasta to sauce and toss to combine. Add mozzarella cheese and let it cook until it gets melted. You may need to add more milk at this point to get the pasta to your desired consistency. Remove from heat. Add spinach and toss until it has wilted. Top with more parmesan cheese if you please.

SPAGHETTI QUICHE

Serving size = 6; cook time = 1 hour

Ingredients

For the spaghetti:

1 tbsp butter plus more for baking dish
1 lb spaghetti
2 c jarred marinara
½ cup freshly grated parmesan

For the quiche:

6 large eggs
½ c heavy cream
½ c whole milk
3 tbsp butter melted
¼ c coarsely chopped fresh basil,
  plus more for garnish
Kosher salt
Freshly cracked black pepper

Directions

Place rack in the center of the oven and preheat to 375 degrees. Generously brush a 10 inch oven safe skillet or 10 inch pie dish with butter and set aside.

Make spaghetti: Boil pasta for about 10 minutes. Drain noodles and rinse with hot water. Return to pot. Add butter and stir until melted. Add marinara and cheese and stir well. Transfer to the prepared baking dish without packing it down too much.

Make the quiche: In a medium bowl whisk together eggs, cream, milk, butter, basil, salt and pepper. Pour mixture over spaghetti. Bake until quiche is set and no longer jiggling, 33 to 35 minutes. Heat broiler and cook quiche until the top is golden up to 5 minutes. Let stand for 15 minutes, then sprinkle with basil and serve. This quiche is delicious served warm or at room temperature or chilled.

EASY SKILLET LASAGNA

Serving size = 6; cook time = 30 minutes

Ingredients
1 lb ground Italian sausage
2 (14 oz) can tomato sauce
1 (14 oz) can diced tomato
½ yellow onion, diced
3 garlic cloves, mined
½ tsp dried basil
½ tsp salt
¼ tsp ground black pepper
¾ lb lasagna noodles, broken
1 c mozzarella cheese, shredded

Toppings:
Mozzarella cheese
Ricotta cheese
Fresh parsley

Directions
Add the ground sausage to a large skillet and cook over medium heat while stirring. Once the sausage is mostly cooked add the diced onion to cook. When the onion is translucent and soft and sausage is cooked through add the minced garlic. Cook for an additional 30 seconds. Add the tomato sauce and diced tomato to the skillet. Stir to combine. Add seasonings and stir.

Break the lasagna noodles over the skillet and add to the sauce. Press the noodles down as much as possible into the sauce. Cover the pan and allow to simmer over medium heat for about

15 to 20 minutes stirring occasionally. Once the noodles are softened add in a cup of mozzarella cheese. Stir to combine. Serve and top with additional mozzarella cheese, ricotta cheese and fresh parsley.

PENNE PASTA WITH A PARMESAN CREAM SAUCE

Serving size = 6-8; cook time = 20 minutes

Ingredients

12 oz penne pasta (use Barilla Pronto for super quick prep)
½ c sundried tomatoes packed in oil, coarsely chopped
8 oz cremini mushrooms, thinly sliced
1 c rotisserie or grilled chicken, shredded
2 c packed baby spinach
½ c parmesan cheese

Parmesan sauce:

1 tbsp olive oil or oil from the sundried tomatoes
3 tbsp unsalted butter
1 tsp minced garlic
3 tbsp white flour
1 c chicken stock or chicken broth; stock has more flavor
1 c milk (1%, 2%, or whole milk; 1% for the lightest version)
½ tsp italian seasoning
5 tbsp parmesan cheese
Salt and pepper to taste
Optional: fresh thyme

Directions

Boil pasta for about 10 minutes. Drain noodles and rinse with hot water. Set aside. In the same pot, over medium heat, add in 1 tablespoon of oil from the sundried tomatoes. Add in the mushrooms and stir for 3 to 4 minutes. Add in the coarsely chopped tomatoes and stir for another 1 to 2 minutes. Dump this mixture on top of the set aside penne.

In the same pot again (return to the burners and put at medium high heat), add 1 more tablespoon sundried tomato oil or olive oil and the butter. Once the butter is melted, stir in the garlic and stir until fragrant, about 30 seconds. Slowly add in the flour, whisking constantly. Whisk for one minute. Slowly add in the chicken broth while whisking and then slowly add in the milk while continuing to whisk.

Increase the heat and allow the mixture to get to a boiling point and then reduce and allow to simmer until thickened stirring occasionally. Add in the Italian seasoning and parmesan cheese and season with salt and pepper to taste. Once the sauce is thickened add back in the pasta and veggie mixture.

Add in the leftover rotisserie chicken (or leftover grilled chicken) and spinach to warm through (get the spinach to wilt) for 2 to 3 minutes over medium high heat. Stir the ingredients until combined and add in the ½ cup parmesan cheese. Stir and enjoy immediately garnished with fresh thyme if desired.

Recipe notes: If you want the dish a little quicker and don't mind dirtying another pot, cook the pasta in one pot and as soon as that's going, start the mushrooms cooking in another pot.

CREAMY PUMPKIN ALFREDO PASTA

Serving size = 4; cook time = 15 minutes

Ingredients
12 oz fettuccine pasta
¼ c butter, divided
1 c heavy cream
¾ c canned pumpkin puree
½ c parmesan cheese, plus more for topping
1 tsp salt, or to taste
½ tsp ground black pepper, or to taste
¼ tsp freshly ground nutmeg

Toppings:
¼ c pine nuts
1 tbsp butter
¼ c fresh sage leaves

Directions
Boil pasta for 10 minutes. Reserve 1 cup pasta water. Drain noodles and rinse with hot water. While pasta is cooking melt butter in large skillet over medium high heat. Add cream and pumpkin puree and whisk until smooth. Add parmesan cheese, salt, pepper and nutmeg and stir until combined. Add drained pasta and toss in sauce. If sauce is too thick add reserved pasta water a tablespoon at a time until smooth; keep warm over low heat while making the topping.

To make the toppings: Add pine nuts to a dry skillet and toast over medium heat 2 to 3 minutes or until nuts are lightly golden brown stirring often. Remove pine nuts from pan and set aside. Melt butter in pan. Add sage leaves and fry 1 to 2 minutes until crispy. Transfer to a paper towel to drain. Serve pasta topped with toasted pine nuts, sage leaves and additional parmesan cheese.

CHEDDAR CARBONARA WITH ROTINI

Serving size = 4; cook time = 15 minutes

Ingredients

Kosher salt
1 lb rotini pasta
8 oz bacon, cut into 1/2" slices
2 lrg eggs at room temperature
2 egg yolks, at room temperature
1 ½ c shredded white cheddar
½ c freshly grated parmesan
Freshly ground black pepper
2 tbsp freshly chopped parsley

Directions

Boil pasta for about 10 minutes. Reserve 1 cup pasta water. Drain noodles and rinse with hot water. Return to pot. In a separate bowl, combine eggs, cheddar, parmesan, salt and pepper and mix well with a fork. Set aside. In a large skillet over medium heat, cook bacon until crispy, 5 to 7 minutes. Using a slotted spoon, transfer bacon to a bowl without draining the fat.

Return skillet to medium heat and add ½ cup pasta water. Turn off heat. Drain pasta and add to skillet. Stir in cheese mixture and parsley, tossing with tongs to evenly coat the pasta and prevent the eggs from scrambling. Add additional pasta water to make a creamy sauce. Before serving mix in parsley. Garnish with bacon and serve immediately.

TURKEY BOLOGNESE

Serving size = 4; cook time = 50 minutes

Ingredients

½ tbsp olive oil
1 - ½ lb lean ground turkey, 93% lean, 7% fat
½ c diced yellow onion
½ c diced carrot
½ c diced celery
6 cloves garlic minced or pressed
3 to 4 tsp dried basil leaves
2 tsp italian seasoning
¼ tsp ground nutmeg
½ tsp salt plus more to taste, I used 1.5 tsp
½ tsp ground black pepper
1 (6 oz) can tomato paste
1 (28 oz) can peeled and crushed tomatoes
1 (8 oz) can tomato sauce
½ c chicken broth
Angel hair pasta, optional

Directions

Heat oil in a stockpot over medium heat. Once hot add in turkey, onion, carrot, celery, garlic, basil, Italian seasoning, nutmeg, salt and pepper. Cook breaking up the turkey as you go until the turkey has cooked through and the carrots are cooking to your liking about 10 minutes. Stir in tomato paste, crushed tomatoes, tomato sauce and chicken broth.

Bring to a simmer stirring regularly. Once simmering reduce heat to low, cover and simmer for 30 minutes. Taste and serve. You can also serve over pasta if you so desire. We used angel hair pasta.

SPAGHETTI WITH PROSCIUTTO, ARUGULA AND FETA

Serving size = 5; cook time = 50 minutes

Ingredients

Marinated feta

8 oz feta cheese (packed in brine)
4 tbsp extra virgin olive oil
½ tsp kosher salt
¼ tsp crushed red pepper flakes
1 clove crushed garlic
A pinch of fresh thyme leaves (optional)

Pasta

1 lb spaghetti or linguini
Kosher salt
2 tablespoons extra olive oil plus extra for adding to cooked pasta
2 large cloves garlic, pressed or finely minced
The zest of 2 limes
3 tbsp small capers, rinsed
1 jalapeno pepper, seeded and finely chopped
6 oz sliced prosciutto, cut into ½ inch dice
5 to 7 oz arugula, leaves stacked and slivered (if using baby arugula, you can chop the leaves or just add them whole)
4 tablespoon fresh lime juice
Kosher salt and fresh ground black pepper to taste

Directions

For the marinated feta: Dice feta into ½ inch cubes and place in a non-reactive bowl or plastic container. Whisk oil, garlic, salt, red pepper flakes and thyme (if using). Toss feta with mixture and let it marinate for at least an hour or up to three days. If marinating for more than an hour cover and store in the fridge.

For the pasta: Boil pasta for about 10 minutes. Drain noodles and rinse with hot water.

Finishing the dish: Meanwhile heat 2 tablespoons oil in a large skillet over medium heat. Add the garlic, lime zest, capers and chopped jalapeno. Cook for a minute or so until the garlic is fragrant. Add the diced prosciutto and cook stirring until the prosciutto is crisp 2 to 3 minutes. Add cooked pasta to the skillet plus 1 tablespoon olive oil. Toss for a minute or two until everything is combined and heated through. Add lime juice and shredded arugula. Toss to combine. Season with salt to taste.

Serve pasta hot in shallow bowls topped with cubes or marinated feta and a sprinkling of sea salt and freshly ground black pepper.

ASPARAGUS, SUNDRIED TOMATOES AND CHICKEN ROTINI PASTA

Serving size = 4; cook time = 30 minutes

Ingredients

12 oz rotini
1 tbsp extra virgin olive oil
1 lb boneless skinless chicken breasts
Kosher salt
Freshly ground black pepper
2 cloves garlic, minced
1 bunch asparagus, stalks trimmed
  and cut into 2″ pieces
½ c roughly chopped sundried tomatoes
¼ c low sodium chicken broth
½ c heavy cream

Directions

Boil pasta for about 10 minutes. Drain noodles and rinse with hot water. Meanwhile in a large skillet over medium high heat heat oil. Add chicken and season with salt and pepper. Cook until golden and no longer pink 8 minutes per side. Transfer chicken to a plate and let rest 10 minutes then slice. Add garlic to skillet and cook until fragrant 1 minute. Add asparagus and sundried tomatoes and cook until asparagus is tender 8 minutes. Pour in broth and heavy cream and bring to a simmer. Add rotini and toss until fully coated.

FOUR CHEESE STUFFED SHELLS

Serving size = 2; cook time = 45 minutes

Ingredients

6 uncooked jumbo pasta shells
½ c shredded part skim mozzarella cheese, divided
¼ c shredded asiago cheese
¼ c ricotta cheese
¼ c 4% cottage cheese
1 tbsp minced chives
1 pkg (10 oz) frozen chopped spinach, thawed and squeezed dry
1 c meatless spaghetti sauce

Directions

Preheat oven to 350 degrees. Boil pasta for about 10 minutes. Meanwhile in a small bowl combine ¼ cup mozzarella cheese, Asiago cheese, ricotta cheese, cottage cheese, chives and ½ cup spinach (save the remaining spinach for another use). Spread ½ cup spaghetti sauce into a shallow 1 ½ qt baking dish coated with cooking spray. Drain pasta and rinse with hot water. Stuff with cheese mixture. Arrange in prepared dish. Top with remaining spaghetti sauce and mozzarella. Cover and bake until heated through 25 to 30 minutes.

Freeze option: Cook unbaked pasta shells. Cover and freeze. To use partially thaw in refrigerator overnight. Remove from refrigerator 30 minutes before baking. Preheat oven to 350 degrees. Bake as directed increasing time as necessary to heat through. For a thermometer inserted in the center of 2 or 3 shells 165 degrees.

SPAGHETTI CARBONARA WITH CHEDDAR

Serving size = 4; cook time = 30 minutes

Ingredients

8 oz spaghetti
8 slices side bacon diced
¾ c thinly sliced green onions
2 eggs lightly beaten
1 ½ c finely shredded Canadian
cheddar cheese
Salt and pepper to taste
Hot chili pepper flakes
½ c finely shredded Canadian cheddar cheese
Chopped fresh parsley

Directions

Boil pasta for about 10 minutes. Drain noodles and rinse with hot water and put in saucepan. Meanwhile cook bacon in a large frypan until crisp. Drain reserving 3 tbsp (45 ml) drippings. Set bacon aside. Return reserved bacon drippings to frypan and cook green onions until tender. Add eggs to hot pasta and toss well to coat. Add 1 ½ cup Canadian Cheddar cheese, cooked bacon and green onion mixture to pasta and continue tossing until cheese melts and coats spaghetti. Add salt, pepper and hot chili pepper flakes to taste. Serve immediately sprinkled with ½ cup (125 ml) Canadian cheddar cheese and parsley.

SAUSAGE AND KALE RAGU OVER SPAGHETTI

Serving size = 6; cook time = 45 minutes

Ingredients
12 oz penne
1 lb Italian sausage, casing removed
½ c dry white wine
2 tbsp olive oil
4 cloves garlic, finely chopped
¼ tsp crushed red pepper flakes
1 (28 oz) can diced tomatoes, drained
3 sprigs fresh basil
¼ c grated Parmesan plus more for serving
4 c baby kale

Directions
Boil pasta for about 10 minutes. Drain noodles and rinse with hot water. Return to the pot. In a medium bowl combine sausage and wine making sure all the wine is incorporated. Let sit at least 5 minutes. Meanwhile heat oil in a large skillet over medium heat. Add garlic and chili flakes and cook until garlic is sizzling about 2 minutes.

Add sausage mixture and cook breaking it up with a spoon into very small pieces until it's no longer pink and half the liquid has evaporated 5 to 7 minutes. Using an immersion or standard blender finely chop tomatoes. Add them to the skillet along with basil. Simmer stirring occasionally 10 minutes. Discard basil and stir in Parmesan. Toss pasta with sauce then fold in kale. Serve with additional Parmesan if desired.

CHEESY RIGATONI WITH ROASTED BROCCOLI, BUTTERNUT SQUASH AND BACON

Serving size = 4-6; cook time = 35 minutes

Ingredients

1 head broccoli, cut into florets, 3 cups
2 c butternut squash, cubed
1 sm red onion, thinly sliced into half moons
¼ c extra virgin olive oil
Kosher salt
6 slices bacon
½ c panko breadcrumbs
12 oz rigatoni
4 oz Fontina cheese, grated or cut into small cubes

Directions

Preheat oven to 425 degrees F. Line two baking sheets with aluminum foil. On one baking sheet arrange broccoli and on the other baking sheet arrange butternut squash and red onion. Drizzle each with 2 tablespoons of olive oil and season generously with salt and pepper tossing to coat. Bake until vegetables are golden and tender 15 to 18 minutes. Bring a large pot of salted water to boil. Meanwhile cook bacon in a large skillet over medium heat until crispy 6 minutes. Transfer to a paper towel lined plate. Let cook then crumble.

Pour all but 2 tablespoons bacon grease from skillet. Add breadcrumbs to pan and cook over medium high heat stirring until golden brown 3 to 4 minutes. Remove from heat and season with salt and pepper. Boil pasta for about 10 minutes. Reserve ½ cup pasta water. Drain noodles and rinse with hot water. Return to the pot. Add Fontina and pasta water stirring until cheese melts. Stir in vegetables and half the bacon. Divide pasta into shallow bowls and top with remaining bacon and a generous sprinkling of breadcrumbs.

PASTA WITH EASY SAUSAGE RAGU

Serving size = 4; cook time = 30 minutes

Ingredients

12 oz penne
1 lb Italian sausage, casings removed
½ c dry white wine
2 tbsp olive oil
4 clove garlic, finely chopped
¼ tsp crushed red pepper flakes
1 - 28 oz can diced tomatoes, drained
3 sprigs fresh basil
¼ c grated Parmesan, plus more for serving
4 c baby kale

Directions

Boil pasta for about 10 minutes. Drain noodles and rinse with hot water. Return to the pot. In a medium bowl combine sausage and wine making sure all the wine is incorporated. Let sit at least 5 minutes. Meanwhile heat oil in a large skillet over medium heat. Add garlic and chili flakes and cook until garlic is sizzling about 2 minutes.

Add sausage mixture and cook breaking it up with a spoon into very small pieces until it's no longer pink and half the liquid has evaporated 5 to 7 minutes. Using an immersion or standard blender finely chop tomatoes. Add them to the skillet along with basil. Simmer stirring occasionally 10 minutes. Discard basil and stir in Parmesan. Toss pasta with sauce then fold in kale. Serve with additional Parmesan if desired.

SPAGHETTI WITH ROASTED CHICKEN AND PEPPERS

Serving size = 6; cook time = 35 minutes

Ingredients

12 oz spaghetti
2 medium boneless skinless chicken breasts (about 1 lb total)
Kosher salt and pepper
1 tbsp olive oil
1 med onion, sliced
1 peppers (1 red and 1 orange), quartered, then sliced crosswise
2 cloves garlic, thinly sliced
¼ c half and half or light or heavy cream
¼ c grated parmesan, plus more for serving
½ c fresh basil, torn
2 oz part skim mozzarella, coarsely grated

Directions

Heat oven to 450 degrees F. Boil pasta for about 10 minutes. Reserve 1 cup pasta water. Drain noodles and rinse with hot water. Return to the pot. Meanwhile heat a large cast iron skillet over medium heat. Season the chicken with ¼ teaspoon each salt and pepper. Add the oil to the skillet, then the chicken placing it on one side and the onions on the other. Cook stirring the onions occasionally until the chicken is browned 4 minutes.

Turn the chicken and toss the onions with the peppers, the garlic, and ¼ teaspoon each salt and pepper. Transfer to oven; roast until the chicken is cooked through and the vegetables are just tender 8 to 10 minutes. Transfer the chicken to a cutting board halve lengthwise then slice crosswise. Toss the pasta with the half and half and Parmesan adding some of the reserved water if the pasta seems dry. Fold in the chicken, roasted vegetables, and basil then serve with the grated mozzarella and extra Parmesan if desired.

SPAGHETTI WITH GRILLED GREENBEANS AND MUSHROOMS

Serving size = 6; cook time = 30 minutes

Ingredients

12 oz spaghetti
10 oz cremini mushroom, sliced in half
1 bunch scallion, slices
Kosher salt
8 oz green beans, slices
2 lemon
Parmesan, grated
1 clove garlic, minced
½ tsp smashed red pepper
1 - ½ tbsp olive oil

Directions

Boil pasta for about 10 minutes. Reserve 1 cup pasta water. Drain noodles and rinse with hot water. Return pasta to pot. Place reserved 1 cup pasta water in it. Place the green beans, mushrooms, scallions into a big bowl. Season with olive oil, salt and smashed red pepper. Toss all and grill it until the vegetables are tender for 5 minutes.

Cut the veggies according to your preference is needed. Make them in bite sized. Mix the vegetables with the lemon zest and mix well. Cut the lemon in half and grill on the both side. Toss the vegetables and the spaghetti with the lemon juice. Mix well. Serve with grated parmesan.

LINGUINE WITH SPINACH BACON AND CLAM SAUCE

Serving size = 4; cook time = 30 minutes

Ingredients

12 oz linguine
6 slices bacon, cut into ½" pieces
2 tbsp extra virgin olive oil
6 cloves garlic, thinly sliced
½ tsp crushed red pepper flakes
¾ c dry white wine
1 (6 oz) can chopped clams
½ c fresh flat leaf parsley, chopped
1 bunch spinach, stems discarded
Grated parmesan, for serving

Directions

Boil pasta for about 10 minutes. Drain noodles and rinse with hot water. Return to the pot. Meanwhile cook the bacon in a large skillet over medium heat until crisp 5 to 6 minutes. Using a slotted spoon transfer to a paper towel lined plate. Discard all but 2 tablespoons of the drippings; add the oil, then the garlic and red pepper. Cook over medium heat stirring occasionally until the garlic is fragrant 1 to 2 minutes.

Add the wine and clams (with their juices) and simmer, stirring occasionally, for 5 minutes. Stir in the parsley. Toss the pasta with the spinach then the sauce and the reserved bacon. Serve with parmesan if desired.

LEMONY SHRIMP & SNOW PEA WITH PASTA

Serving size = 6; cook time = 30 minutes

Ingredients

1 - ¾ c uncooked gemelli or spiral pasta
2 tbsp olive oil, divided
2 c fresh snow peas
1 lb uncooked shrimp (26-30 per pound), peeled and deveined
3 garlic cloves, minced
¾ tsp salt, divided
¼ tsp plus 1/8 teaspoon pepper, divided
1 c grape tomatoes, halved

Dressing

¼ cup lemon juice
2 tbsp chopped fresh parsley
2 tbsp olive oil
2 garlic cloves, minced
2 tsp grated lemon zest
Additional grated lemon zest and chopped fresh parsley, optional

Directions

Boil pasta for about 10 minutes. Reserve ½ cup pasta water. Drain noodles and rinse with hot water. Meanwhile in a large cast iron or other heavy skillet heat 1 tablespoon oil over medium heat. Add peas. Cook and stir until crisp tender 2 to 3 minutes. Remove and keep warm. In same pan heat remaining oil over medium high heat. Add shrimp. Cook and stir until shrimp turn pink 2 to 3 minutes. Add garlic ½ teaspoon salt and ¼ teaspoon pepper. Cook and stir 1 minute longer.

Add pasta to shrimp mixture. Stir in peas and tomatoes. In a small bowl whisk lemon juice, parsley, oil, garlic, lemon zest and remaining salt and pepper until blended. Pour over shrimp mixture. Toss to coat adding enough reserved pasta water to moisten pasta. If desired sprinkle with additional lemon zest and parsley.

SPRING CARROT PENNE WITH BACON AND PEAS

Serving size = 4; cook time = 40 minutes

Ingredients

12 oz penne rigate
1 tbsp olive oil
½ small yellow onion, thinly sliced
8 oz carrots, thinly sliced
2 c low sodium chicken broth
2 lrg egg yolks
Kosher salt
4 slices of thick cut bacon (about 8 oz) cut into ¼ in pieces
½ c dry white wine
1 c (about 5 oz) shelled English peas or frozen peas

Directions

Boil pasta for about 10 minutes. Reserve 2 cups pasta water. Drain noodles and rinse with hot water. Return to the pot. Meanwhile heat oil in a large skillet on medium. Add onion and cook stirring occasionally until tender 4 minutes. Add carrots and broth. Cover and bring to a boil then reduce heat and simmer until carrots are very tender about 15 minutes. Strain reserving liquid. Add carrots and onion to a blender and puree adding just enough vegetable liquid to get the blender moving (about ¼ cup) until smooth. Add egg yolks and 1/5 tsp salt and puree to combine.

Clean skillet and return to medium. Add bacon and cook until browned and crisp 6 to 10 minutes. Transfer to a paper towel lined plate and discard drippings. Add wine to skillet and bring to a simmer scraping up any browned bits. Simmer until reduced to about 2 tablespoon then add peas and ½ cup reserved vegetable liquid. Bring to a simmer and cook until peas are just tender and bright green about 2 minutes if fresh 30 seconds if frozen. Toss pasta with carrot sauce. Fold in pea mixture and bacon adding reserved pasta water if sauce seems too thick.

RAVIOLI WITH CREAMY MUSHROOMS AND ASPARAGUS

Serving size = 4; cook time = 35 minutes

Ingredients

1 (9 ounce) package fresh cheese ravioli
2 tablespoons unsalted butter
2 c sliced mushrooms (cremini or baby bellas work well)
1 tablespoon olive oil
5 ounces fresh asparagus
Juice of 1 lemon
1 tablespoon fresh parsley, roughly chopped
½ c grated parmesan cheese
¼ tsp fresh ground black pepper

Directions

Boil pasta for about 10 minutes. Drain noodles and rinse with hot water. While you are waiting for it to boil prep the asparagus by breaking off the woody ends (bend the spear and it should naturally break where it needs to). Chop the parsley and grate the cheese. Melt the butter in a large pan over medium heat. Add the mushrooms and toss them around.

Let them cook for just a couple of minutes until they start to brown. Add the asparagus and the olive oil to the pan and toss everything around. Cook it all together tossing frequently until the asparagus is tender. Once the pasta is cooked transfer it (using a spider or large slotted spoon) to the pan. Squeeze the lemon juice over everything in the pan and give it all a good toss to ensure it's coated. Sprinkle in the parsley and toss again. Add the parmesan cheese to the pan and give everything another good toss. Sprinkle the pepper over the top and serve.

Recipe notes: I subbed fresh ravioli for frozen tortellini (all I had on hand) firm-cooked to package directions) halved the amount of lemon juice and added a pinch of garlic powder. My husband and I just stared at each other in silence the whole time we ate. Cannot believe how easy this was to make because it seriously tasted like a fine dining entrée.

SPAGHETTI WITH BACON AND PARMESAN BRUSSEL SPROUTS

Serving size = 3-4; cook time = 30 minutes

Ingredients

12 oz spaghetti
1 lb small Brussel sprouts, halved (quartered if large)
1 large clove garlic, thinly sliced
1 tbsp olive oil
Pinch red pepper flakes
Kosher salt
Pepper
3 strips bacon, cut into ½ inch pieces (about 1 ½ oz)
½ c grated parmesan, plus more for serving
1 small lemon

Directions

Heat oven to 425 degrees F. Boil pasta for about 10 minutes. Reserve ¾ cup pasta water. Drain noodles and rinse well. Return to the pot. Meanwhile on a large baking sheet toss Brussel sprouts and garlic with oil, red pepper flakes and ¼ teaspoon each salt and pepper. Scatter bacon over the top and roast for 15 minutes. Increase heat to broil. Sprinkle sprouts with ¼ cup Parmesan and toss to combine then broil on the top rack until bacon is crisp and Brussels sprouts are golden brown and tender 1 to 2 minutes.

Finely grate lemon zest onto pasta then squeeze in juice and toss to coat. Toss with remaining ¼ cup Parmesan adding some reserved cooking liquid if pasta seems dry. Serve Brussels sprout mixture on spaghetti with additional Parmesan if desired.

SHRIMP PUTTANESCA

Serving size = 4; cooking time = 30 minutes

Ingredients

2 tbsp olive oil
1 lb uncooked shrimp (31-40 per pound), peeled and deveined
¾ to 1 teaspoon crushed red pepper flakes, divided
¼ tsp salt
1 small onion, chopped
2 to 3 anchovy fillets, finely chopped
3 garlic cloves, minced
2 c grape tomatoes or small cherry tomatoes
½ c dry white wine or vegetable broth
1/3 c pitted Greek olives, coarsely chopped
2 teaspoon drained capers
Sugar to taste
Chopped fresh Italian parsley
Hot cooked spaghetti, optional

Directions

In a large skillet heat 1 tablespoon oil. Sauté shrimp with ½ teaspoon pepper flakes until shrimp turn pink 2 to 3 minutes. Stir in salt. Remove from pan. In same pan heat remaining oil over medium heat. Sauté onion until tender about 2 minutes. Add anchovies, garlic and remaining pepper flakes. Cook and stir until fragrant about 1 minute.

Stir in tomatoes, wine, olives and capers; bring to a boil. Reduce heat then simmer uncovered until tomatoes are softened and mixture is thickened 8 to 10 minutes. Stir in shrimp. Add sugar to taste; sprinkle with parsley. If desired serve with spaghetti.

ROTINI WITH BRUSSEL SPROUTS, CHILE PEPPERS AND PANCETTA

Serving size = 2; cook time = 20 minutes

Ingredients

Sea Salt
8 oz rotini
2 tbsp extra virgin olive oil, more for drizzling
3 oz pancetta, diced
1 lrg rosemary sprig
6 garlic cloves, smashed and peeled
1 jalapeno or serrano chile, thinly sliced (or substitute 1 lrg pinch crushed red pepper flakes)
Fresh ground black pepper
8 oz Brussel sprouts, thinly sliced
2 tsp butter
Fresh lemon juice, for serving
Freshly grated pecorino cheese (optional)

Directions

Boil pasta for about 10 minutes. Drain noodles and rinse with hot water. Meanwhile heat large sauté pan over high heat and add the olive oil. When oil is hot add the pancetta and rosemary and sauté until the fat on the pancetta starts to turn translucent and very lightly brown about 1 minute. Add the garlic, chile and freshly ground black pepper to taste and sauté until garlic and pancetta turn richly brown about 3 minutes.

Add the brussel sprouts, a large pinch of salt and a splash of water to pan and sauté until sprouts just start to soften about 2 minutes. Spread sprouts mixture in and press down to flatten. Let it sear for a minute then stir it up and repeat. This helps brown the sprouts. Add the butter and sauté for another minute. Drain rotini and add it to pan with brussel sprouts mixture. Cook tossing until everything is well mixed. Spoon into pasta bowls and top with a drizzle of oil and lemon juice and a little cheese if you like.

CHEESY SHELLS AND GREENS

Serving size = 4; cook time = 30 minutes

Ingredients

12 oz medium pasta shells
1 tbsp unsalted butter
2 tbsp all-purpose flour
1 – ¼ c whole milk
1 tbsp Dijon mustard
½ tsp freshly grated or ground nutmeg
Pinch cayenne (optional)
6 oz extra-sharp cheddar
Kosher salt and pepper
1 bunch spinach, thick stems discarded

Directions

Boil pasta for about 10 minutes. Drain noodles and rinse with hot water. Meanwhile melt the butter in a large pot over medium heat. Add the flour and cook stirring for 2 minutes; whisk in the milk. Cook stirring occasionally until slightly thickened 5 minutes. Whisk in the mustard, nutmeg, cayenne (if using), 1 cup cheddar, ½ tsp salt and ¼ tsp pepper. Add the pasta and spinach and toss to combine. Heat broiler. Transfer the mixture to a 1 ½ qt broiler-proof baking dish or four 12 oz ramekins. Sprinkle with the remaining ½ cup Cheddar and broil until golden brown 2 to 4 minutes.

Recipe notes: Add a crispy bread crumb topping to this dish: Pulse 4 slices bread in a food processor to form coarse crumbs. Stir in ¼ cup finely chopped flat leaf parsley and 2 tbsp olive oil. Sprinkle over the pasta before broiling.

CHICKEN WITH LEMON LEEK LINGUINE

Serving size = 4 (serving - 1 chicken breast half and 1 cup pasta mixture); cook time = 30 minutes

Ingredients

6 oz uncooked linguine
4 (6 oz) skinless, boneless
  chicken breast halves
½ tsp salt, divided
¼ tsp black pepper
¼ c all-purpose flour
3 tbsp butter, divided
3 garlic cloves, thinly sliced
1 leek, trimmed, cut in half lengthwise,
  and thinly sliced (1 ½ cups)
½ c fat free, lower sodium chicken broth
2 tbsp fresh lemon juice
2 tbsp chopped fresh flat leaf parsley

Directions

Boil pasta for about 10 minutes. Drain noodles and rinse with hot water. Keep warm. Place chicken between 2 sheets of heavy duty plastic wrap and pound to an even thickness using a meat mallet or small heavy skillet. Sprinkle chicken with ¼ teaspoon salt and pepper. Place flour in a shallow dish and dredge chicken in flour shaking to remove excess. Heat 1 tablespoon butter in a large nonstick skillet over medium high heat.

Add chicken and cook 3 minutes on each side or until done. Remove chicken from pan and keep warm. Melt 1 tablespoon butter in skillet over medium high heat. Add garlic, leek, and remaining ¼ teaspoon salt. Sauté 4 minutes. Add broth and juice. Cook 2 minutes or until liquid is reduced by half. Remove from heat and stir in remaining 1 tablespoon butter. Add pasta to leek mixture and toss well to combine. Serve chicken over pasta mixture. Sprinkle with parsley.

SKILLET MAC AND CHEESE

Serving size = 4; cook time = 20 minutes

Ingredients

2 c uncooked elbow macaroni (about 8 oz)
2 tbsp butter
2 tbsp all-purpose flour
1 - ½ c half and half cream
¾ lb process cheese (Velveeta), cubed
Optional toppings: fresh arugula, halved cherry tomatoes and coarsely ground pepper

Directions

Boil pasta for about 10 minutes. Drain noodles and rinse with hot water. Meanwhile in a large cast iron or other heavy skillet melt butter over medium heat. Stir in flour until smooth; gradually whisk in cream. Bring to a boil stirring constantly. Cook and stir until thickened about 2 minutes. Reduce heat; stir in cheese until melted. Add macaroni and stir until heated through. Top as desired.

BROCCOLI AND CHEESE STUFFED SHELLS

Serving size = 6; cook time = 50 minutes

Ingredients

1 container (15 oz) ricotta cheese
1 pkg (10 oz) chopped frozen broccoli cuts, thawed and well drained
1 c shredded mozzarella cheese (about 4 oz)
1/3 c grated parmesan cheese
¼ tsp ground black pepper
18 cooked jumbo shell shaped pasta, drained
1 jar (23 - ¾ oz) Prego Chunky Garden Combination Italian Sauce

Directions

Stir the ricotta, broccoli, ½ cup of the mozzarella cheese, parmesan cheese and black pepper in a medium bowl. Spoon about 2 tablespoons of the cheese mixture into each shell. Spread 1 cup of the sauce in a 13 x 9 x 2 inch shallow baking dish. Place the filled shells on the sauce. Pour the remaining sauce over the shells. Sprinkle with the remaining mozzarella cheese. Bake at 375 degrees F for 1 hour or until it's hot and bubbling.

BAKED SPAGHETTI

Serving size = 6; cook time = 1 hour

Ingredients

1 pkg (16 oz) spaghetti
1 lb ground beef
1 medium onion, chopped
1 ½ jar (24 oz) pasta sauce
½ tsp seasoned salt
2 large eggs
1/3 c grated Parmesan cheese
5 tbsp butter, melted
2 c Daisy 4% cottage cheese
4 c shredded part-skim mozzarella cheese
Chopped fresh basil, optional

Directions

Preheat oven to 350 degrees. Boil pasta for about 10 minutes. Drain noodles and rinse with hot water. Meanwhile in a large skillet cook beef and onion over medium heat until beef is no longer pink and onion is tender 6 to 8 minutes breaking up beef into crumbles; drain. Stir in pasta sauce and seasoning salt; set aside. In a large bowl whisk the eggs, Parmesan cheese and butter. Add spaghetti to egg mixture and toss to coat.

Place half of the spaghetti mixture in a greased 13 x 9 inch or 3 qt baking dish. Top with half of the cottage cheese, meat sauce and mozzarella cheese. Repeat layers. Place baking dish on a rimmed baking sheet. Cover and bake for 40 minutes. Uncover; bake until cheese is melted, 20 to 25 minutes longer. If desired sprinkle with basil.

Recipe notes: This yummy baked spaghetti casserole will be requested again and again for potlucks and family gatherings.

CROCK POT SPAGHETTI AND MEATBALLS

Serving size = 6; cook time = 2 hours

Ingredients

1 (24 oz) jar spaghetti sauce
4 c water (vegetable or beef broth can also be used)
1 (16 oz) (1 lb) box spaghetti
1 (26 oz) bag frozen meatballs (24 count)
Olive oil

Optional sauce ingredients:

1 ½ tsp Italian seasoning
1 ½ tsp minced garlic
1 ½ tsp dried basil (or 2-3 leaves, fresh basil, torn)

Directions

In a 6 quart slow cooker pour in jarred spaghetti sauce. Then add 4 cups of water. I just use the spaghetti jar and fill it up about one and half times to get 4 cups. Instead of water try using vegetable broth or beef broth for a kick of flavor. Add in minced garlic, Italian seasoning and basil. Break the spaghetti noodles in half and put in a large Ziploc bag. Coat the spaghetti noodles with a drizzle of olive oil.

Close the bag and gently move the noodles around until they are all coated. Then remove noodles from bag and put noodles on top of sauce mixture and gently push them down so they are slightly in the sauce. Then top with frozen meatballs. No need to stir these in. Just put them right on top. Cover and cook on low for about 2 to 5 hours (until noodles are soft and meatballs are heated through). Then give it all a gentle stir to combine and serve.

ONE POT CHILI MAC AND CHEESE

Serving size = 3-4; cook time = 30 minutes

Ingredients

1 tsp olive oil
1 lb ground beef extra lean
1 large onion chopped
3 cloves garlic minced
¼ tsp cayenne pepper
1 tsp cumin ground
1 tbsp chili powder
1 tsp black pepper ground
1 tsp salt
1 c black beans drained and rinsed
1 c kidney beans drained and rinsed
26 oz diced tomatoes (1 can)
4 c chicken broth low sodium
10 oz elbow macaroni pasta uncooked
2 c cheddar cheese shredded
2 tbsp parsley chopped

Directions

In a large sauce pan or dutch oven heat the olive oil over medium high heat. Add the ground beef and cook until no longer pink. Since I'm using extra lean ground beef there's no need to drain the fat but if you're using fatter ground beef drain whatever fat there is. Stir in the onion and garlic and cook for about 3 minutes or until the onion softens and becomes translucent and the garlic is aromatic. Add the cayenne pepper, cumin, chili powder, salt and pepper and stir.

Add the black beans, kidney beans, tomatoes, chicken broth and elbow pasta. Stir everything together and bring to a boil. Turn down the heat to a simmer. Cover the pot and cook for about 9 to 12 minutes or until the elbow macaroni is cooked. Stir in 1 cup of the shredded cheese then sprinkle the remaining cheddar cheese over the top. Cover the pot for about 1 minute just until the cheese melts. Garnish with fresh parsley and serve.

Recipe notes: The elbow macaroni can be replaced with any shape pasta. Store in an airtight container and keep refrigerated for up to 4 days. If freezing allow the dish to fully cool in a shallow container before placing in the freezer for up to 3 months. Please keep in mind that nutritional information is a rough estimate and can vary greatly based on products used.

CACIO E PEPE BAKED GNOCCHI

Serving size = 3-4; cook time = 40 minutes

Ingredients

12 oz gnocchi
1/3 c shredded pecorino romano
1/3 c shredded asiago
1/3 c shredded parmesan
2 tbsp butter
1 ½ tsp cracked black pepper

Directions

Bring a large pot of salted water to boil. Boil gnocchi in water until they float to the surface. Drain noodles and rinse with hot water. In a large skillet melt butter and add black pepper. Add gnocchi to the skillet and toss to coat. Mix cheese together and toss gnocchi with ¾ cup of cheese (reserve remaining ¼ cup of cheese). Put gnocchi in a small baking dish. Top gnocchi with remaining cheese. Heat broiler on high and bake gnocchi for several minutes or until top has melted and has begun to brown. Remove from heat and enjoy.

SMOKED SALMON PASTA

Serving size = 4; cook time = 20 minutes

Ingredients

10 oz pasta, gluten free if needed (we like linguine but any pasta will work)
5 oz baby spinach
2 tablespoons olive oil
1 medium onion, minced
3 garlic cloves, minced
10 oz smoked salmon (see notes)
2 c cherry tomatoes, cut in half
1 c canned artichoke hearts (cut in half if large)
2/3 c sour cream or plain yogurt
¼ c lemon juice (from 1 lemon)
2 tablespoons capers
A pinch of chili flakes
Salt and pepper, to taste
1 tablespoon fresh dill (or 1 teaspoon dried)

Directions

Bring a large pot of water to a boil over high heat. Add the pasta and cook until al dente. Reserve 1 cup of the pasta water then drain the pasta and put it back into the pot. Place the spinach on top of the pasta. Heat the oil in a large pan over medium high heat. Add the onion and cook for 2 minutes until it is transparent. Add the garlic and cook for 1 minute.

Break the smoked salmon into pieces and add it to the pan along with the cherry tomatoes, artichoke hearts, sour cream, lemon juice, capers, chili flakes and ½ cup of the pasta water. Bring the pan to a boil and stir until everything is creamy and mixed together. Season to taste with salt and pepper then mix in the dill. Pour the smoked salmon sauce into the pasta pot and mix everything together. If needed add a splash more of pasta water to loosen the pasta.

FIVE-CHEESE ZITI AL FORNO

Serving size = 6; cooking time = 1 hour 15 minutes

Ingredients

1 ½ pounds (about 7 ½ cups) ziti or small tube pasta
2 jars (24 oz each) marinara sauce
1 jar (15 oz) Alfredo sauce
2 c shredded part-skim mozzarella cheese, divided
½ c reduced-fat ricotta cheese
½ c shredded provolone cheese
½ c grated Romano cheese

Topping:
½ c grated parmesan cheese
½ c panko bread crumbs
3 garlic clove, minced
2 tbsp olive oil
Minced fresh parsley or basil, optional

Directions

Preheat oven to 350 degrees. Boil pasta for about 10 minutes. Drain noodles and rinse with hot water. Meanwhile in a large saucepan combine marinara sauce, alfredo sauce, 1 cup mozzarella, ricotta, provolone and romano cheeses. Heat over medium heat until sauce begins to simmer and cheeses are melted. Stir in cooked pasta; pour mixture into a greased 13x9 inch baking dish. Top with remaining 1 cup mozzarella cheese. In a small bowl stir together parmesan, bread crumbs, garlic and olive oil; sprinkle over pasta.

Bake uncovered until mixture is bubbly and topping is golden brown 45 minutes to 1 hour. Let stand 10 minutes before serving. Garnish with fresh parsley or basil if desired.

Freeze option: Cool unbaked casserole; cover and freeze. To use partially thaw in refrigerator overnight. Remove from refrigerator 30 minutes before baking. Preheat oven to 350 degrees. Cover casserole with foil; bake 50 minutes. Uncover; bake until heated through and a thermometer inserted in center reads 165 degrees 15 to 20 minutes longer.

CRISPY BAKED SHRIMP SCAMPI

Serving size = 6; cooking time = 20 minutes

Ingredients

2 lb shrimp, peeled, deveined
and tails on or off
2 tbsp freshly squeezed lemon juice
2 tbsp white wine (optional sub with
extra lemon juice or chicken stock)
1 brown shallot, minced
1/3 c melted butter, divided
Salt and pepper, to taste
1/3 c Panko breadcrumbs
4 cloves garlic, minced
2 tbsp grated parmesan cheese
½ tsp crushed red pepper flakes
or more, to taste
¼ c fresh chopped parsley leaves
Lemon wedges to serve
Spaghetti pasta, optional

Directions

Heat oven to 425 degrees F (220 degrees C). Combine shrimp, lemon juice, white wine, shallots, 2 tablespoons of melted butter, 1 teaspoon salt and ¼ teaspoon pepper in a skillet or baking dish. Mix well to coat shrimp. Optional: Starting from the outer edge of your skillet or dish, arrange the shrimp in a single layer towards the center of the pan. Set aside.

In a small bowl, combine the remaining melted butter, breadcrumbs, garlic, parmesan cheese, red pepper flakes and 2 tablespoons of the chopped parsley; mix well. Sprinkle the breadcrumb mixture over the shrimp and bake for 12 minutes, or until hot and bubbling, and the shrimp are just cooked through. Change oven settings to broil or grill for a further minute or so until the top is crispy and golden.

Garnish with remaining parsley, squeeze over a drizzle of lemon juice and serve with lemon wedges. You can serve over pasta or rice if you wish.

RAVIOLI LASAGNA

Serving size = 6; cook time = 1 hour 10 minutes

Ingredients

1 lb ground beef
½ medium onion, chopped
Kosher salt
Freshly ground black pepper
2 cloves garlic, minced
1 (32 oz) jar marinara
16 oz whole milk ricotta
1 large egg
1 c freshly grated Parmesan, divided
¼ c freshly chopped basil, plus
    more for garnish
1 tsp garlic powder
2 oz (12 oz) packages frozen cheese ravioli
2 c shredded mozzarella

Directions

Preheat oven to 350 degrees and grease a 9 x 13 inch baking dish with cooking spray. Warm a large, nonstick skillet over medium heat and add ground beef and onion. Season with salt and pepper and cook until beef is browned and onion is soft about 10 minutes then drain fat and return to skillet. Stir in garlic and marinara then reduce heat and simmer for flavors to meld 5 minutes. Meanwhile in a medium bowl add ricotta, egg, ¼ cup Parmesan, basil, garlic powder and season with salt and pepper.

Stir to combine. Spread 1/3 of the meat sauce into prepared pan. Top with a single layer of ravioli, half of the remaining meat sauce, half of the ricotta mixture, and half of the mozzarella and remaining Parmesan. Repeat layers ending with cheeses. Cover pan loosely with aluminum foil and bake for 30 minutes. Remove foil and bake until golden bubbly 15 minutes more. Sprinkle with remaining basil and serve.

PERFECT CHICKEN ALFREDO

Serving size = 4; cooking time = 30 minutes

Ingredients

1 lb boneless skinless chicken thighs, (or breast)
Salt and pepper, to season
2 tbsp olive oil, divided
1 onion, diced
4 cloves garlic, minced (or 1 tablespoon minced garlic)
½ c dry white wine, optional
8 oz brown mushrooms, sliced
2 c chicken broth, or stock
1 ½ c heavy cream, divided (thickened cream, light cream, evaporated milk can also be used)
Extra salt and pepper, to taste
8 oz dry pasta, penne or fettuccini
1 ½ c freshly grated parmesan cheese
Fresh chopped parsley, to garnish

Directions

Season chicken thighs with salt and pepper. Heat half of the oil in a large pot over medium high heat. Add the chicken thighs and sear on both sides until golden brown and cooked through. Remove chicken and set aside. Add the remaining oil in the pot. Fry onion until transparent stirring occasionally (about 2 minutes). Sauté the garlic until fragrant (30 seconds) then add in the white wine and allow to reduce to half (about 4 to 5 minutes).

Add the mushrooms and cook for about a minute while stirring occasionally. Pour in broth and 1 cup of cream (or evaporated milk); season with salt and pepper. Bring to a gentle simmer then add the pasta. Mix well and reduce the heat to a slow simmer while stirring occasionally until pasta is al dente (about 15 minutes). Cook pasta longer if you like. Stir in the parmesan cheese until it melts through the sauce.

Remove from heat immediately and slowly add in ¼ to ½ cup remaining cream if sauce is too thick for your liking. Adjust salt and pepper to your taste. Slice the chicken into strips and stir through the pasta. Garnish with fresh parsley and extra parmesan if desired.

Recipe notes: You can dice the chicken first, sear, then leave in the pot to continue cooking with the rest of the ingredients on from Step 2 if you wish. Use a good quality dry white wine. Pinot Grigio, Sav Blanc or Chardonnay. Substitute heavy cream (or thickened cream) with half and half, light cream or evaporated milk. If the sauce is too thick add hot water in ¼ cup increments until smooth. Use freshly grated parmesan cheese. Remove the pot off of the stove while there's still a bit of sauce in the bottom of the pot and the pasta is cooked al dente (firm to the bite). The sauce begins to evaporate quite quickly while it sits waiting to be served and as you mix it through adjusting salt and pepper.

LEMON RICOTTA PASTA

Serving size = 4; cook time = 15 minutes

Ingredients

Kosher salt
1 lb short, ribbed pasta, like gemelli or penne
1 cup whole milk ricotta (8 oz)
1 c freshly grated Parmesan or pecorino (2 oz), plus more for serving
1 tbsp freshly grated lemon zest plus ¼ cup lemon juice (from 1 to 2 lemons)
Black pepper
Red pepper flakes, for serving
¼ c thinly sliced or torn basil leaves, for serving (optional)

Directions

Bring a large pot of salted water to a boil. Add the pasta and cook according to package instructions until al dente. Reserve 1 cup pasta cooking water then drain the pasta. In the same pot make the sauce: Add the ricotta, Parmesan, lemon zest and juice, ½ teaspoon salt and ½ teaspoon pepper and stir until well combined. Add ½ cup pasta water to the sauce and stir until smooth. Add the pasta and continue to stir vigorously until the noodles are well coated. Add more pasta water as needed for a smooth sauce. Divide the pasta among bowls and top with some of the sauce that's pooled at the bottom of the pot. Garnish with grated Parmesan, black pepper, red pepper flakes and basil, if using.

LASAGNA ROLL UPS

Ingredients

1 pkg frozen chopped spinach,
defrosted and squeezed dry
2 c mozzarella cheese, shredded
1 ½ c ricotta cheese or cottage cheese
¾ c parmesan cheese, shredded, divided
1 egg
9 lasagna noodles, cooked and drained
1 lb lean ground beef
1 onion chopped
1 clove garlic
2 c pasta sauce

Directions

Preheat oven to 350 degrees. Brown ground beef, onion and garlic until no pink remains. Drain and stir in pasta sauce. Cook and drain lasagna noodles according to package direction. In a small bowl combine egg, spinach, cottage cheese, ½ cup parmesan cheese and 1 cup mozzarella cheese. Lay out cooked lasagna noodles and divide ricotta cheese mixture over noodles. Roll jelly roll style.

Half of the meat sauce in a 9 x 13 dish. Place roll ups in dish and top with remaining sauce. Cover with foil and bake 30 minute. Remove foil and top with remaining cheeses. Bake an additional 10 minutes or until cheese is melted.

Serving size = 6-8; cook time = 1 hour 15 minutes

CHICKEN SPAGHETTI

Serving size = 6-8; cook time = 1 hour 5 minutes

Ingredients

8 oz spaghetti, cooked
2 c chicken, shredded
1 onion, chopped
1 clove garlic, minced
½ green bell pepper, chopped
1 tsp Italian seasoning
¼ c butter
¼ c flour
1 c flour
1 c chicken broth
¾ c light cream
14 oz diced tomatoes, drained
  or tomatoes with chilies
Salt and pepper
½ c parmesan cheese, shredded
2 c sharp cheddar cheese, divided

Directions

Preheat oven to 375 degrees F. Boil pasta for about 10 minutes. Drain noodles and rinse with hot water. Set aside. Cook onion, garlic and bell pepper in butter until tender. Add flour and seasonings. Cook 1 to 2 minutes. Stir in broth and cream a little bit at a time until smooth. Cook until thick and bubbly. Remove from heat. Add parmesan cheese and 1 cup cheddar. Mix until smooth and melted. Season with salt and pepper to taste.

Combine spaghetti, chicken, cream sauce and canned tomatoes mix well. Spread in a greased 9 x 13 dish. Top with remaining cheddar cheese and bake 25 to 30 minutes or until hot and bubbly.

SEARED SALMON OVER 50/50 SPAGHETTI WITH ARUGULA AND WALNUT PESTO

Serving size = 2; cook time = 40 minutes

Ingredients

Arugula-walnut pesto

1 garlic clove
¼ c raw walnuts
1 1/3 heaping cups arugula
½ c extra virgin olive oil
2 tbsp freshly grated parmesan
Salt and pepper to taste

50/50 pasta:

2 tbsp extra virgin olive oil
2 tbsp unsalted butter, melted
4 oz cherry tomatoes
3 garlic cloves
3 thyme sprigs
6 oz dry spaghetti
2 medium zucchini, ends trimmed and peeled with a julienne peeler

Salmon:

2 tbsp extra virgin olive oil
2 (4 oz) boneless salmon fillets
Salt and pepper to taste

Garnish:

Freshly grated parmesan

Directions

Preheat oven to 375 degrees F.

For pesto: Place garlic, walnuts and pepper flakes into a food processor and pulse until evenly ground. Add arugula. With the motor running slowly drizzle in oil until fully blended. Fold in parmesan and salt and pepper. Set aside. In a shallow baking dish combine oil, butter, tomatoes, garlic, and thyme and place into the oven. Roast tomatoes for 15 minutes. Remove from oven and sprinkle with salt and pepper. Set aside.

Pasta: Boil pasta for about 10 minutes. Add the zucchini and cook for an additional 30 seconds. Drain pasta and zucchini into a colander and rinse with hot water and set aside.

For salmon: Pour oil into a skillet and place oven on medium high heat. Season salmon fillets with salt and pepper. Place each fillet skin side up and sear for 2 to 3 minutes or until the fillets lift up easily from the skillet. Flip and sear for an additional 2 to 3 minutes. Transfer skillet to the oven and roast for 7 to 8 minutes or until each fillet has just cooked through.

To assemble: Scoop pesto into a large mixing bowl and top with pasta and zucchini blend. Toss together until pasta and zucchini are well coated. Divide pasta mixture between 2 serving bowls and top with roasted tomatoes and a piece of salmon. Finish each dish with freshly grated Parmesan and serve.

SPAGHETTI QUICHE

Serving size = 6; cook time = 55 minutes

Ingredients

1 tbsp unsalted butter, plus more for the baking dish
1 lb spaghetti
2 c jarred marinara sauce
½ c grated parmesan cheese

For the quiche:

6 lrg eggs
½ c heavy cream
½ cup whole milk
3 tbsp unsalted butter, melted
¼ c fresh basil, coarsely chopped, plus more for garnish
1 ½ tsp salt
¾ tsp fresh cracked black pepper

Directions

Place a rack in the center of the oven and preheat to 375 degrees. Generously brush a 10 inch oven safe skillet or 10 inch pie dish with butter and set aside. Boil pasta for about 10 minutes. Drain noodles and rinse with hot water. Add 1 tablespoon butter and stir until melted. Add the marinara sauce and cheese and stir well. Transfer to the prepared baking dish without packing it down too much.

In a medium bowl whisk together the eggs, cream, milk, butter, basil, salt and pepper. Pour the mixture over the spaghetti. Bake 30 to 35 minutes until the quiche is set and no longer jiggling. Turn on the oven broiler and heat the quiche under the broiler up to 5 minutes until the top is golden. Let stand for 15 minutes. Sprinkle with basil before serving. This quiche is delicious served warm at room temperature or chilled.

PERFECT BUTTERED NOODLES

Serving size = 6; cook time = 20 minutes

Ingredients

1 (14.5 oz) can chicken broth
1 cup water
1 chicken or beef bouillon cube
1 stick butter, divided
1 (12 oz) package wide egg noodles
¼ tsp garlic powder
Freshly ground black pepper
Chopped parsley

Directions

Combine broth, water, bouillon cube, and half the stick of butter in a large nonstick skillet. Bring to a boil. Add noodles and cook, stirring frequently for about 8 minutes. Turn the heat down so the liquid does not boil vigorously and evaporate too quickly. Add more water if necessary. Add garlic powder and remaining butter and stir well. Remove from heat and season with pepper and sprinkle with parsley.

Recipe notes: The finished noodles will be fairly salty. If you want them less salty, use reduced sodium broth or a reduced sodium bouillon cube.

Directions

In a large pot over medium high heat heat olive oil and cook garlic, onions and carrots until softened 4 to 5 minutes. Add celery and tomato paste. Season with salt and pepper and cook 1 more minute. Add broth and ½ cup of water. Bring to a boil. Add ravioli and cook according to package directions. Fold in spinach and parsley and heat until warmed. Serve immediately.

RAVIOLI SOUP

Serving size = 6; cook time = 30 minutes

Ingredients

1 tsp extra virgin olive oil
2 cloves garlic, minced
½ c diced onion
2 carrots, diced
2 celery stalks, diced
3 tbsp tomato paste
Kosher salt
Freshly ground black pepper
32 oz Swanson chicken broth
1 (9 oz) package cheese ravioli
5 oz baby spinach
½ c chopped fresh parsley

PASTA FAGIOLI

Serving size = 4-6; cook time = 30 minutes

Ingredients

1 tbsp olive oil
1.2 onion 3 cloves garlic, chopped
1 med celery stalk, chopped
1 med carrot, finely chopped
1 - 15 oz can cannellini beans
15 oz can tomato sauce or crushed tomatoes
1 lrg bay leaf
1 tbsp basil
1 tbsp parsley
1 tsp oregano
2 - 14 oz each cans fat free chicken broth
or vegetable broth for vegetarians
2 cups water
Kosher salt and pepper to taste
6 oz dry gemelli pasta or other small pasta
Grated parmesan cheese for topping optional

Directions

In a deep pot sauté onion and garlic in olive oil over medium heat. Blend the cup of beans with one can water in electric blender until almost smooth. Add blended beans to pan then add the can of tomato sauce, celery, carrots, chicken broth, basil, bay leaf, parsley, oregano, salt and pepper. Add 1 cup water and bring to a boil. Simmer covered for 20 minutes stirring occasionally. Add pasta and cook uncovered until pasta is al dente according to pasta directions. Ladle soup into bowls and top with grated cheese (optional).

CAJUN CHICKEN LASAGNA

Serving size = 12; cook time = 1 hour 45 minutes

Ingredients

1 (16 oz) package lasagna noodles
1 lb andouille sausage, quartered lengthwise and sliced
1 lb skinless, boneless chicken breast halves – cut into chunks
2 tsp Cajun seasoning
1 tsp dried sage
½ c chopped onion
½ c chopped celery
¼ c chopped red bell pepper
1 tbsp finely chopped garlic
2 (10 oz) containers alfredo sauce, divided
1 ½ c shredded mozzarella cheese
½ c grated parmesan cheese

Directions

Preheat oven to 325 degrees F (165 degrees C). Boil pasta for about 10 minutes. Drain noodles and rinse with hot water. In a large skillet over medium high heat combine sausage, chicken, Cajun seasoning and sage. Cook until chicken is no longer pink and juices run clear about 8 minutes. Remove meat from skillet with a slotted spoon and set aside. Sauté onion, celery, bell pepper and garlic until tender. Remove from heat and stir in cooked meat and one container alfredo sauce.

Lightly grease a 9 x 13 inch baking dish. Cover bottom with 4 lasagna noodles. Spread with ½ of the meat mixture. Repeat layers and cover with a layer of noodles. Spread remaining alfredo sauce over top. Top with mozzarella cheese and sprinkle with parmesan cheese. Bake in preheated oven for 1 hour. Let stand 15 minutes before serving.

BAKED CREAMY GARLIC RIGATONI

Serving size = 4; cook time = 30 minutes

Ingredients

Kosher salt
1 lb rigatoni
1 (15 oz) can cannellini beans, rinsed and drained
1 tbsp extra virgin olive oil
5 cloves garlic, minced
1- ½ tsp fresh thyme leaves, divided
½ tsp crushed red pepper flakes
Freshly ground black pepper
1 c freshly grated pecorino, divided
1 c freshly grated parmesan, divided

Directions

Boil pasta for about 10 minutes. Reserve 1 cup pasta water. Drain noodles and rinse with hot water. Return to pot. Using a blender puree beans with 1 cup fresh water until smooth. Set aside. Position rack to the top third of the oven and turn on broiler. In a large cast iron skillet over medium high heat heat oil and sauté garlic until softened.

Add 1 cup pasta water, bean mixture, 1 teaspoon thyme, red pepper flakes and seafood with salt and pepper. Bring to a boil and simmer on low for 5 minutes. Mix in ½ cup pecorino and ½ cup parmesan. Fold in sauce over pasta until just combined. Transfer back to cast iron skillet. Sprinkle remaining cheese evenly over pasta. Broil until golden brown and bubbling about 10 minutes. Garnish with remaining thyme leaves and serve immediately.

FOUR CHEESE ANGEL HAIR PASTA

Serving size = 2; cook time = 30 minutes

Ingredients

1 tbsp butter
1 tbsp olive oil
2 cloves garlic (minced)
2 oz cream cheese (softened to room temperature)
¼ c Asiago cheese
¾ c Parmesan cheese
½ c Pecorino Romano cheese
½ c heavy cream
8 oz cooked spaghetti (reserve ¼ cup of the pasta water)
Salt and pepper to taste
1 tsp finely chopped Italian parsley

Directions

Gather the ingredients. Boil pasta for about 10 minutes. Reserve ¼ cup pasta water. Drain noodles and rinse with hot water. In a large skillet at high temperature heat the butter and olive oil. Reduce the heat to low and add the minced garlic. Cook until fragrant (be careful not to brown the garlic as it will change the flavor). Using a whisk stir in the heavy cream and gradually add the cream cheese, romano, parmesan ½ cup and asiago cheeses until you achieve a thick sauce consistency.

Add the cooked spaghetti and reserve pasta water to the sauce. Season with salt and pepper and cook for another 2 minutes tossing the pasta until it is completely coated with the sauce. Leave in the skillet or transfer to a serving dish. Top with chopped parsley and the remaining ¼ cup of parmesan cheese. Serve the pasta in warm bowls to keep the cheese sauce creamy while eating. Enjoy!

SLOPPY JOE MAC AND CHEESE

Serving size = 4-6; cook time: 30 minutes

Ingredients
For the sauce
¾ c tomato sauce
2 tbsp dark brown sugar
1 tbsp tomato paste
2 tsp Worcestershire sauce
½ tsp kosher salt
¼ tsp ground black pepper

For the Pasta and Remainder of Dish:
2 c dry rotini (or any spiral-shaped) pasta
1 tbsp vegetable oil
¾ c diced onion
1 med green bell pepper, diced (about ½ cup)
2 cloves garlic, minced
½ lb ground beef
1 c freshly grated sharp cheddar cheese

Directions
For the sauce: In a medium bowl whisk together all the ingredients for the sauce and set aside.
For the pasta and the remainder of the dish: Boil pasta for about 10 minutes. Drain noodles and rinse with hot water. In a large skillet over medium high heat heat up the vegetable oil. Add the green bell pepper and garlic. Sauté until fragrant and softened about 5 minutes. Add the ground beef to the skillet and break it up with your spatula or wooden spoon. Cook until ground beef is thoroughly cooked through about 5 to 7 minutes. Add the sauce to the skillet. Then add the pasta (drained of excess water) and the cheese on top. Turn the heat down to medium low and toss the mixture until the cheese has melted and the ingredients are evenly coated and distributed throughout. Serve warm.

SKILLET MEAT AND CHEESE PASTA

Serving size = 4-6; cook time = 1 hour 15 minutes

Ingredients

8 oz ½ a box, medium pasta,
such as shells or rotini
1 to 2 tbsp extra virgin olive oil
1 lb ground beef
1 tsp garlic powder
½ tsp crushed red pepper flakes
Kosher salt and ground black pepper
One 20 oz jar pasta sauce
8 oz about 2 cups shredded
sharp cheddar cheese

Directions

Heat the oven to 400 degrees. Boil pasta for about 10 minutes. Drain noodles and rinse with hot water. Meanwhile heat the oil in a large cast iron skillet over medium heat. Add the ground beef and season with garlic powder, crushed red pepper flakes, salt and pepper and cook breaking apart with a wooden spoon until the beef is cooked through 5 to 7 minutes.

Add the pasta sauce and simmer reducing the heat as needed for 15 minutes. Taste and adjust the seasonings to your liking. Add the cooked pasta along with about ½ cup of the cheese to the sauce and stir to combine. Sprinkle the remaining cheese on top and bake in the oven until the cheese has melted and the sauce is gently bubbling about 15 minutes. Let cool slightly before serving.

SHRIMP AND BROCCOLI FETTUCCINE

Serving size = 4-6; cook time = 30 minutes

Ingredients

Kosher salt
1 lb fettucine
Extra virgin olive oil, for drizzling
1 head broccoli, cut into florets
2 tbsp butter
2 cloves garlic minced
¼ c chicken broth
Freshly ground black pepper
1 lb shrimp peeled and deveined
2 c tomato sauce
½ c heavy cream
¼ c chopped fresh parsley

Directions

Boil pasta for about 10 minutes. In the last minute of cooking add broccoli. Meanwhile in a large skillet over medium heat melt butter and sauté with garlic for 2 minutes. Add chicken broth, 1 teaspoon salt and ½ teaspoon pepper. Bring to a simmer and toss in shrimp. Sauté until pink about 3 minutes. Transfer shrimp to a bowl and set aside. Stir in tomato sauce and heavy cream. Simmer on low for 5 minutes. Toss in pasta and broccoli until well combined and add back shrimp. Stir until warmed through. Garnish with parsley and serve immediately.

SPAGHETTI WITH KALE PESTO AND MEATBALLS

Serving size = 6-8; cook time = 30 minutes

Ingredients

16 oz dried spaghetti
1 lb sausage meat
1 bunch Tuscan kale, remove the tough stems and chop the leaves finely
½ c walnuts
½ c grated parmesan
½ c and 1 tbsp extra virgin olive oil
¼ c freshly squeezed lemon juice
2 tsp grated lemon zest
2 small garlic cloves, minced
Salt and pepper to taste
Garnish additional parmesan

Directions

First make the pesto by pulsing kale, walnuts, lemon juice, zest and garlic in a food processor. Then add ¼ cup of olive oil and parmesan and pulse again to thick paste. Add the remaining ¼ cup of olive oil as the pesto blends. Season with salt and pepper then set aside.

Second make the meatballs. Roll the sausage meat into meatballs (each meatballs should be about 1 inch in diameter). Then heat the one tablespoon of olive oil in a skillet. Cook the meatballs in it for 10 to 12 minutes or until browned. Transfer the meatballs to a plate lined with paper towels to blot the excess oil. Throw out the remaining oil in the pan and wipe it clean.

Third boil pasta for about 10 minutes. Reserve ¼ cup pasta water. Drain noodles and rinse with hot water. Return the pasta to the pot then add the pesto and pasta water. Stir for about one to two minutes over low heat. When the pasta is evenly coated add the meatballs and toss until the meatballs are warm as well. Serve immediately with more grated parmesan for garnish.

Recipe notes: This dish is not only green for the eyes it's also green for the belly. By making the pesto using kale instead of basil you can get more fiber and nutrition making it a healthier alternative to the classic spaghetti and meatballs.

SLOW COOKER CHILI MAC AND CHEESE

Serving size = 6-8; cook time = 4 hours

Ingredients

1 lb very lean ground beef
1 sm onion, chopped
4 cloves garlic, minced
1 (30 oz) can chili beans in chili sauce or 2 (15 to 16 oz) cans chili beans in chili sauce
1 (28 oz) can crushed tomatoes
1 (15 oz) can diced tomatoes
2 c beef broth
1 tbsp chili powder
½ tsp cumin
Salt and pepper to taste
8 oz elbow macaroni, uncooked
Desired toppings: cheddar, sour cream, green onions, corn chips

Directions

Brown ground beef and drain grease. Add to slow cooker and stir in remaining ingredients except for the pasta. Cover and cook for 4 hours on high or 8 hours on low. In the last 15 minutes of cooking stir in the uncooked pasta and cover. Stir and test to see if pasta is to your liking. However even with the slow cooker off the pasta will continue to cook just from the heat of the chili. Unless your pasta is really chewy or crunchy I strongly suggest only cooking it for the last 15 minutes of cook time. Serve immediately with desired toppings.

Recipe notes: If you wish not to brown the beef first place ground beef in the bottom of your slow cooker and break into smaller chunks.

PENNE WITH ROASTED SUMMER VEGETABLES AND RICOTTA SALATA

Serving size = 6; cook time = 30 minutes

Ingredients

1 sm eggplant, diced
1 md zucchini, diced
½ pt grape tomatoes, halved
3 tbsp extra virgin olive oil
Kosher salt
Freshly ground black pepper
12 oz penne pasta
¾ c grated ricotta salata, plus more for serving
¼ c finely chopped fresh basil, plus more for serving

Directions

Preheat oven to 425 degrees. Arrange eggplant on one half of baking sheet and zucchini on other half. On another baking sheet arrange tomatoes. Drizzle vegetables with olive oil and season with salt and pepper. Toss to combine then roast vegetables until golden about 20 minutes stirring halfway through. Meanwhile boil pasta for about 10 minutes. Reserve 1 cup pasta water. Drain noodles and rinse with hot water. Return to pot.

Remove vegetable from oven and scrape into pasta using spatula. Add ricotta salata and ½ cup pasta water stirring to combine. (Add an additional ¼ cup liquid to create a creamier pasta if desired). Stir in chopped basil and season with salt and pepper. Serve pasta in bowls. Garnished with more ricotta salata and basil.

SPAGHETTI WITH LEMON ARUGULA AND PROSCUTTO

Serving size = 4; cook time = 35 minutes

Ingredients

12 oz spaghetti
1 lemon (juice and zest of)
2 lemons, quartered
1 tbsp butter
½ c parmesan, freshly grated
1 tsp red pepper flakes
3 oz prosciutto
4 c arugula
½ tsp salt
¼ tsp pepper

Directions

Boil pasta for about 10 minutes. Reserve 1 cup pasta water. Drain noodles and rinse with hot water. Return to pot. Place lemon zest and juice in a small bowl. Thinly slice remaining ½ lemon into half moon and remove seeds then set aside. Add lemon juice, zest, butter, Parmesan and ½ cup pasta water to pot then stir gently to combine adding additional pasta water until creamy. Add red pepper flakes, prosciutto, arugula and lemon slices and toss until arugula just begins to wilt. Season with salt and pepper. Garnish with parmesan and serve.

Directions
Cook and stir chicken in large nonstick skillet on medium heat 8 to 10 minutes or until done. Add milk, water and macaroni; stir. Bring to boil and simmer on medium low. Cook until macaroni is tender stirring occasionally. Stir in cheese sauce and broccoli. Cook and stir 5 minutes or until heated through.

SKILLET MAC AND CHEESE WITH CHICKEN AND BROCCOLI

Serving size = 4; cook time = 30 minutes

Ingredients
1 lb boneless skinless chicken breasts, cut into bite – size pieces
1 c each milk and water
1 pkg (14 oz) KRAFT deluxe macaroni and cheese dinner made with 2% milk
1 pkg (10 oz) frozen broccoli florets, thawed

CHEESY SUN DRIED TOMATO PENNE PIE

Serving size = 4; cook time = 35 minutes

Ingredients
Kosher salt
1 box penne
½ c sun dried tomatoes with oil
2 ½ c crushed tomatoes
1 clove garlic, chopped
Freshly ground black pepper
½ c freshly chopped parsley, divided
¼ c extra virgin olive oil
2 ½ c shredded gruyere cheese divided

Directions
Preheat oven to 375 degrees. Lightly grease a 9" or 10" pie dish and set aside. Bring an 8 quart stock pot of water to a boil and generously season with salt. Boil pasta for about 10 minutes. Drain noodles and rinse with hot water. Add back to stock pot. Meanwhile in the bowl of a food processor add sun dried tomatoes, crushed tomatoes, garlic, salt and pepper, ¼ cup parsley and olive oil. Pulse until well combined.

Pour sauce into stock pot and mix with pasta. Stir in 1 ½ cup cheese then pour pasta mixture into pie pan. Top with remaining cup cheese and bake until cheese is melty 25 minutes. Garnish with remaining parsley and serve immediately.

SPRING ASPARAGUS AND MUSHROOM GEMELLI

Serving size = 4; cook time = 25 minutes

Ingredients

Kosher salt
1 lb gemelli
3 tbsp extra virgin olive oil
1 lb baby bella mushrooms,
    sliced into ¼″ pieces
2 cloves garlic, minced
Freshly ground black pepper
1 c vegetable stock
1 lb asparagus, chopped into 1″ pieces
2 tbsp butter
1 c freshly grated parmesan,
    plus more for garnish
1 c freshly grated fontina cheese
½ c parsley leaves

Directions

Boil pasta for about 10 minutes. Reserve 1 cup pasta water. Drain noodles and rinse with hot water. Return to pot. Meanwhile in a large skillet over medium high heat heat oil. Add mushrooms and spread in an even layer. Cook for 3 minutes before stirring to let the mushrooms brown. Add garlic and season with salt and pepper and cook 2 minutes more.

Add stock and asparagus then using a wooden spoon scrape bottom of pan to remove the browned garlic and mushrooms. Bring to a boil and simmer for 5 minutes. Add butter, pasta and both cheeses then gently mix with tongs (If the pasta seems dry slowly add reserved pasta water) until desired consistency is reached. Serve in skillet or transfer pasta to a platter and top with grated Parmesan and a drizzle of olive oil and parsley. Serve immediately.

PENNE PASTA WITH CREAMY TOMATO AND MEAT SAUCE

Serving size = 3-4; cook time = 50 minutes

Ingredients

1 tbsp extra virgin olive oil
½ c chopped onion
1 sm carrot (peeled and finely shredded)
1 rib celery (finely chopped)
¼ c water
8 oz lean ground beef (or more for a meatier sauce)
1 sm clove garlic (crushed and minced)
¼ c dry white wine
1 tbsp all-purpose flour
1/3 c tomato paste
1 ½ cups milk, divided
¾ tsp salt
½ tsp freshly ground black pepper
½ tsp dried leaf oregano, crumbled
½ tsp dried leaf basil
12 oz penne pasta (or ziti)
3 tbsp grated Parmesan cheese (plus more for serving)

Directions

In a large skillet or sauté pan heat oil over medium heat. Add the onion and cook frequently stirring until softened. Stir in shredded carrot, chopped celery and ¼ cup water. Cook until vegetables are tender and liquid has evaporated about 5 minutes longer. Add the ground beef to the vegetables and cook until it has browned and is no longer pink for about 4 minutes. Add garlic and cook for 1 minute longer stirring constantly.

Add the wine and cook until the liquid has evaporated about 5 minutes. Stir in the flour and cook stirring for 2 minutes. Add the tomato, ½ cup of milk, salt, pepper and oregano. Reduce heat and simmer frequently stirring until the milk has been absorbed. Continue cooking until the sauce has thickened. Gradually adding the remaining 1 cup of milk. Cook over low heat for about 15 to 20 minutes longer.

Meanwhile boil pasta for about 10 minutes. Drain noodles and rinse with hot water. Transfer sauce to a large serving bowl. Add the penne pasta and Parmesan cheese; toss penne pasta gently. Sprinkle some extra parmesan cheese over the bowl of pasta and serve more at the table.

BUCATINI ALL'AMATRICIANA

Serving size = 4; cook time= 45 minutes

Ingredients

2 tbsp extra virgin olive oil
4 oz thinly sliced guanciale, pancetta, or chopped unsmoked bacon
½ tsp crushed red pepper flakes
½ tsp freshly ground black pepper
¾ c minced onion
2 cloves garlic, minced
1 28 oz can peeled tomatoes with juices, crushed by hand
Kosher salt
12 oz dried bucatini or spaghetti
¼ c finely grated Pecorino (about 1 oz)

Directions

Heat oil in a large heavy skillet over medium heat. Add guanciale and sauté until crisp and golden about 4 minutes. Add pepper flakes and black pepper; stir for 10 seconds. Add onion and garlic; cook stirring often until soft about 8 minutes. Add tomatoes and reduce heat to low. Cook stirring occasionally until sauce thickens 15 to 20 minutes. Boil pasta for about 10 minutes. Reserve 1 cup pasta water. Drain noodles and rinse with hot water. Add drained pasta to sauce in skillet and toss vigorously with tongs to coat. Add ½ cup of the reserved pasta water and cook until sauce coats pasta and pasta is al dente about 2 minutes. (Add a little pasta water if sauce is too dry.) Stir in cheese and transfer pasta to warmed bowls.

FETTUCINE WITH TOMATOES AND CRISPY CAPERS

Serving size = 6; cook time = 25 minutes

Ingredients

½ c extra virgin olive oil
¼ c small capers (drained and patted dry)
¼ c cornstarch
4 oil-packed anchovies (chopped)
2 lrg garlic cloves (thinly sliced)
2 oz thinly sliced prosciutto (cut into 1-inch wide ribbons)
2 tomatoes (coarsely chopped)
½ tsp crushed red pepper
1 tbsp thinly sliced basil
1 lb fettucine
Freshly grated Parmigiano-Reggiano cheese (for serving)

Directions

In a large skillet heat the olive oil. In a small bowl toss the capers with the cornstarch and transfer to a sieve; shake off the excess cornstarch. Add the coated capers to the oil and fry over high heat tilting and gently shaking the pan until the capers are crispy and golden about 3 minutes. Drain the capers reserving 2 tablespoon of the oil in the skillet. Spread the capers on a paper towel-lined plate.

Add the anchovies and garlic to the skillet and cook over high heat stirring until the garlic is golden and the anchovies dissolve about 3 minutes. Add the prosciutto separating the ribbons and cook until lightly browned about 1 minutes. Add the tomatoes and crushed red pepper and cook just until the tomatoes begin to break down about 3 minutes. Stir in the basil.

Meanwhile boil pasta for about 10 minutes. Reserve ½ cup pasta water. Drain noodles and rinse with hot water. Return to pot along with the water and pour the sauce over top. Toss over high heat just until the sauce is thickened about 2 minutes. Serve the pasta in bowls and garnished with the crispy capers. Pass the grated cheese at the table.

PENNE WITH CREAMED LEEK AND SPINACH

Serving size = 4; cook time = 30 minutes

Ingredients

¾ lb penne
1 ½ tbsp. extra virgin olive oil
1 lrg leek
1 c heavy cream
4 c packed baby spinach
½ c lightly packed basil leaves
Kosher salt and freshly ground pepper

Directions

Boil pasta for about 10 minutes. Drain noodles and rinse with hot water. Meanwhile in a large deep skillet heat the olive oil. Add the leek and cook over moderate heat until softened about 10 minutes. Add the cream and simmer over moderate heat until slightly thickened about 5 minutes. Add the spinach and cook until wilted about 2 minutes. Add the cooked fusilli to the skillet and toss over moderately low heat until coated with the leek sauce about 1 minute. Remove from the heat. Add the chopped basil and toss. Season with salt and pepper. Spoon fusilli into bowls and serve.

PENNE RIGATE WITH BRUSSEL SPROUTS AND GORGONZOLA

Serving size = 4; cook time = 20 minutes

Ingredients

2 tbsp extra-virgin olive oil
1 sm red onion (thinly sliced)
1 lb brussels sprouts (trimmed, loose outer leaves reserved and sprouts thinly sliced)
1 long red fresh chile (halved, seeded and sliced crosswise / 4inch thick)
1 tsp chopped thyme
Salt and freshly ground pepper
½ lb penne rigate
4 oz gorgonzola cheese, preferably dolce latte (crumbled)

Directions

In a large deep skillet heat the olive oil. Add the onion and cook over moderately high heat stirring for 3 minutes. Add the sliced brussel sprouts, chile and thyme and season with salt and pepper. Cover and cook over moderate heat stirring occasionally until the sprouts are just tender about 3 minutes. Add the reserved spout leaves and cover. Remove from the heat. Meanwhile boil pasta for about 10 minutes. Reserve ¾ cup pasta water. Drain noodles and rinse with hot water. Add the pasta to the skillet along with cooking water and cook over moderate heat stirring to coat the pasta with the vegetables. Season with salt and pepper. Transfer the pasta to bowls and top with the Gorgonzola. Serve right away.

CHEESY MIXED PASTA CASSEROLE WITH MUSHROOMS

Serving size = 6; cook time = 1 hour

Ingredients

½ c dried porcini mushrooms (½ oz)
1 lb mixed short pasta shapes such as ziti
6 tbsp unsalted butter
4 tbsp all-purpose flour
3 cups milk
2 tbsp heavy cream
½ lb shiitake mushroom (stems discarded and caps quartered)
½ lb white button mushrooms (stems trimmed and caps quartered)
Kosher salt and freshly ground pepper
4 ½ oz fontina cheese (1 cup plus 2 tablespoons coarsely grated)
½ c finely grated parmigiana reggiano cheese

Directions

In a heatproof glass measuring cup cover dried porcini mushrooms with 1 cup of boiling water. Let stand until the mushrooms are soft about 20 minutes. Drain and reserve ¾ cup of the porcini soaking liquid. Finely chop the mushrooms. Preheat the oven to 375 degrees. Boil pasta for about 10 minutes. Drain noodles and rinse with hot water. Meanwhile in a large saucepan melt 4 tablespoons of the butter.

Add the flour and cook over moderate heat stirring until smooth about 1 minutes. Whisk in the reserved porcini liquid and the milk. Bring to a simmer and cook over moderately low heat until thickened about 5 minutes. Stir in the cream and chopped porcini mushrooms. Scrape into a large bowl. In a large skillet melt the remaining 2 tablespoon of butter.

Add the mushrooms and season with salt and pepper. Cook over moderately high heat until browned in spots about 5 minutes. Add the mushrooms to the porcini sauce. Stir in the pasta and fontina cheese and season with salt and pepper. Scrape the pasta into an 8 ½ x 12 inch baking dish. Sprinkle with parmigiano-reggiano and bake for about 35 minutes until golden and bubbly. Let stand 5 minutes before serving.

BAKED FOUR CHEESE SPAGHETTI

Serving size = 8; cook time = 55 minutes

Ingredients

1 ½ lb spaghetti
½ lb imported Fontina (2 cups coarsely shredded)
½ lb mozzarella (2 cups coarsely shredded)
½ lb Gruyere (2 cups coarsely shredded)
¼ lb Gorgonzola dolce (crumbled)
Salt and freshly ground pepper

Directions

Preheat the oven to 350 degrees. Lightly butter a 9 x 13 inch baking dish. Boil pasta for about 10 minutes. Drain noodles and rinse with hot water. In a large bowl toss the Fontina with the mozzarella and Gruyere. Spread one third of the spaghetti in the prepared baking dish in an even layer. Sprinkle 1/3 of the mixed cheeses and half of the Gorgonzola over the spaghetti and season with salt and pepper.

Repeat with another layer of spaghetti, mixed cheeses, gorgonzola and salt and pepper. Top with the remaining spaghetti and mixed cheeses. Bake the spaghetti in the center of the oven until the top is golden brown for 40 minutes or until bubbly. Let cool slightly before cutting into squares and serve.

PASTA WITH SUN DRIED TOMATO AND ALMOND PESTO

Serving size = 4; cook time = 20 minutes

Ingredients

½ c drained oil packed sun dried tomatoes (I reserved and used the oil, it's got good flavor)
1/3 c salted roasted almonds I used Marconi almonds, skin on
1 lrg garlic clove sliced
½ c extra virgin olive oil plus more for drizzling
Salt and freshly ground pepper
½ c fresh bread crumbs
12 oz spaghetti I used whole grain
1/3 c chopped parsley plus more for garnish

Directions

In a food processor pulse the tomatoes, almonds and garlic. Add ¼ cup of the oil and puree. Season with salt and pepper. In a skillet toast the bread crumbs in 2 tablespoons of the oil stirring until golden. Transfer the crumbs to a plate; season with salt and pepper. Boil pasta for about 10 minutes. Reserve ½ cup of pasta water. Drain noodles and rinse with hot water. Return to pot. Toss the pasta with the pesto, parsley, some of the reserved cooking water and remaining 2 tablespoons of oil until the sauce clings to the pasta. Transfer the pasta to bowls. Sprinkle with the bread crumbs and little more parsley. Drizzle with olive oil.

THE BEST THREE CHEESE SKILLET LASAGNA

Serving size = 4; cook time = 30 minutes

Ingredients

1 (28 oz) diced tomatoes with basil and garlic
1 med onion minced, 1/4" pieces
1 tablespoon olive oil
2 cloves garlic minced
½ tsp salt
1 lb hot italian sausage
1 tsp italian seasoning
10 dry lasagna noodles broken
into 2-inch pieces
1 - 8 oz tomato sauce not pasta sauce
½ c parmesan cheese freshly grated
4 oz whole milk ricotta cheese
8 oz fresh mozzarella cheese

Directions

In a 4 cup measuring cup pour in the tomatoes and add enough water to bring the total to 4 cups. Set aside. Heat a 12" skillet over medium heat and add the olive oil. Add the onion and ½ tsp salt and cook the onions until translucent. About 5 minutes. Add the garlic and cook 30 seconds. Add the sausage and cook crumbling and breaking it up until no pink remains. If your meat is very fatty drain off what you can. Add the Italian seasoning and stir well.

Add the broken lasagna noodles to the skillet. Add the diced tomatoes and tomato sauce. Cover and bring to a simmer (not a rolling boil) and cook stirring occasionally 20 minutes. Your sauce should look watery after 15 minutes of cooking. If yours is very dry add ½ cup water and stir it in. After the 20 minutes remove the lid and stir in the parmesan cheese. Add the ricotta in drops and slice the fresh mozzarella. Lay slices on top and cover with the lid and place the skillet off the heat for 5 minutes for the cheese to soften or place it under the broiler just to melt the cheese.

CHEESE TORTELLINI WITH WALNUT PESTO

Serving size = 4; cook time = 15 minutes

Ingredients

1 c walnuts
1 c lightly packed flat leaf parsley with thick stems removed
2 clove garlic
3 tbsp grated parmesan cheese
½ c olive oil
½ tsp salt
¼ tsp fresh ground black pepper
1 lb fresh or frozen cheese tortellini
1 tbsp butter

Directions

In a food processor or blender pulse the walnuts, parsley, garlic, Parmesan, oil, salt and pepper to a coarse puree. Boil pasta for about 10 minutes. Reserve ½ cup pasta water. Drain noodles and rinse with hot water. Return to pot. Toss with ¼ cup of the reserved pasta water, the walnut pesto and the butter.

If the pasta seems dry add more of the reserved pasta water. Sprinkle with additional Parmesan and pass more at the table. Wine recommendation: Look for a crisp, acidic white wine to cut through the richness of the walnuts. A sauvignon blanc from either California or New Zealand would be suitable.

Recipe notes: Here's one of the quickest pesto sauces you'll come across. It's a perfect match for cheese tortellini but you can use other tortellini such as mushroom or meat instead. The pesto is also great with just about any plain pesto.

MOSTACCIOLI

Serving size = 8; cook time = 1 hour 5 minutes

Ingredients

1 lb uncooked mostaccioli
1 (½ lb) bulk Italian sausage
1 jar (28 oz) meatless spaghetti sauce
1 lrg egg, lightly beaten
1 carton (15 oz) ricotta cheese
2 c shredded part skim mozzarella cheese
½ c grated Romano cheese

Directions

Boil pasta for about 10 minutes. Drain noodles and rinse with hot water. Crumble sausage into a dutch oven. Cook over medium heat until no longer pink; drain. Stir in spaghetti sauce and pasta. In a large bowl combine the egg, ricotta cheese and mozzarella cheese. Spoon half of the pasta mixture into a greased shallow 3 quart baking dish. Layer with cheese mixture and remaining pasta mixture.

Cover and bake at 375 degrees for 40 minutes or until a thermometer reads 160 degrees. Uncover; top with Romano cheese. Bake 5 minutes longer or until heated through.

Recipe notes: Even though we're not Italian this rich cheesy pasta dish is a family tradition for holidays and special occasions. I was delighted the first time I tried this mostaccioli recipe it has all the flavor of lasagna without the work of layering the ingredients. Try it. I'm sure it'll become one of your family's favorite too.

CHORIZO-POACHED SHRIMP PASTA

Serving size = 4; cook time = 40 minutes

Ingredients

1 c extra virgin olive oil
4 oz Spanish chorizo (cut into ½ inch pieces)
1 lb shrimp (large shelled and deveined)
4 cloves garlic (large thinly sliced)
Kosher salt
Pepper
12 oz fettucine pasta
1 pint cherry or grape tomatoes
(halved if large)
1 c basil (plus more for garnish torn)

Directions

In a medium saucepan cook the olive oil and chorizo over moderate heat stirring occasionally until the chorizo is tender about 10 minutes. Using a slotted spoon transfer to a small bowl. Add the shrimp, garlic and a generous pinch of salt to the saucepan and cook over low heat stirring occasionally until the shrimp are cooked through 8 to 10 minutes. Using a slotted spoon transfer the shrimp and garlic to the bowl with the chorizo. Reserve the oil. Meanwhile boil pasta for about 10 minutes. Drain noodles and rinse with hot water.

In the pot combine the tomatoes and ½ cup of the reserved chorizo oil; discard the remaining oil. Cook over moderately high heat stirring occasionally until the tomatoes just start to soften about 3 minutes. Add the shrimp mixture and the pasta and cook tossing until hot and the pasta is coated in a light sauce about 2 minutes. Season generously with salt and pepper then stir in the torn basil. Transfer to bowls. Garnish with more basil and serve right away.

CREAMY BAKED PASTA WITH GRUYERE AND PROSCIUTTO

Serving size = 6; cook time = 35 minutes

Ingredients

1 (16 oz) package gemelli pasta
16 oz Gruyere cheese finely shredded (about 4 cups)
3 oz Parmigiano-Reggiano cheese finely shredded (about 1 ¼ cup)
3 c heavy cream
1 ½ tsp kosher salt
1 tsp freshly grated whole nutmeg
Thinly sliced prosciutto for serving

Directions

Boil pasta for about 10 minutes. Drain noodles and rinse with hot water. Return to pot. Toss together gruyere and parmigiano-reggiano in a medium bowl and set aside. Preheat broiler to high with oven rack in middle of oven. Bring heavy cream and salt to a simmer in a large saucepan over high heat.

Reduce heat to medium; stir in nutmeg and simmer stirring often 2 minutes. Remove from heat. Stir in 4 ½ cups of the cheese mixture in small batches stirring until cheese is melted after each addition. Stir in cooked pasta. Spoon pasta mixture into a 2 ½ quart broiler proof baking dish and top with remaining 1 cup cheese mixture. Broil in preheated oven until cheese is melted and golden brown 3 to 5 minutes. Let stand 10 minutes before serving. Serve with thinly sliced prosciutto.

CRAB MACARONI GRATIN

Serving size = 6-8; cook time = 30 minutes

Ingredients

8 oz uncooked medium pasta shells (about 3 cups)
4 oz white cheddar cheese, finely shredded (about 1 cup)
3 oz Gruyere cheese, finely shredded (about ¾ cup)
3 oz Parmigiano-Reggiano cheese, grated (about ¾ cup)
2 ½ c heavy cream
1 med garlic glove, finely chopped
12 oz fresh Dungeness crabmeat (about 2 cups), picked over
5 tbsp thinly sliced fresh chives, divided
Fine sea salt to taste

Directions

Boil pasta for about 10 minutes. Drain noodles and rinse with hot water. Meanwhile toss together cheddar, gruyere and parmigiano-reggiano until well combined; set aside 1 cup cheese mixture. Preheat broiler to low with oven rack in top third of oven. Bring cream just to a boil in a large saucepan over medium high. Reduce heat to low; add garlic and gently simmer stirring often 2 minutes. Stir in cooked pasta and return to a gently simmer over medium. Cook stirring often 1 minute.

Reduce heat to medium low. Stir in cheese mixture in three additions (about 1 ½ cups at a time) until cheese is melted after each addition. Gently stir in crab and ¼ cup chives. Season to taste with salt. Spoon pasta mixture into an 8 x 6 x 2 inch broiler proof baking dish. Set on a rimmed baking sheet. Top with reserved 1 cup cheese mixture in an even layer. Broil in preheated oven until cheese is golden brown and crusty 5 to 7 minutes rotating as needed for even browning. Let stand 5 to 10 minutes and sprinkle with remaining 1 tablespoon chives.
Notes: My mid December birthday marks the start of crab season. Several years ago I started inviting friends over under the disguise of a birthday party but really it's a celebration of the season the past year and yes the fresh

catch of the best crab on the planet. My guest list included too many friends to fit around my dining table so we're packed like sardines snug in the candle lit room with magnums of Champagne and a pile of steaming whole crabs to be cracked and dipped in melted butter. It's messy and a bit chaotic but fancy at the same time. I'd have it no other way. I like to choose a theme for the annual menu usually inspired by a travel experience I had that year. Last year I visited one of my favorite cities, Florida not once but twice so it seemed fitting to entertain come December. The crab was cooked with creole seasoning in the boil classic and delicious but the surprise hit was the macaroni au gratin served with it.

CREAMY LEMON PASTA

Serving size = 4; cook time = 20 minutes

Ingredients
12 oz wide egg noodles
Zest and juice of 2 lemons; zest cut
in very thin strips 1 inch long
1 c heavy cream
Kosher salt to taste
Lots of freshly ground black pepper

Directions
Boil pasta for about 10 minutes. Drain noodles and rinse with hot water. Just before noodles are done in a small saucepan combine the lemon zest, cream and salt and pepper. Cook for 2 minutes or until cream comes to a boil. Pour cream mixture over drained noodles and add the lemon juice. Stir to coat. Cook over medium heat stirring until all the liquid is absorbed about 1 to 2 minutes. Season with additional pepper if desired.

Recipe notes: This astonishingly delicious pasta dish is surprisingly easy to make. Just combine the zest of two lemons, heavy cream, salt and pepper in a saucepan and let it come to a boil. Pour over freshly cooked egg noodles and add fresh lemon juice and toss. Cook for a couple minutes until the sauce has thickened slightly and coats the noodles in a rich creamy lemony brightness. It's luxurious weeknight cooking at its best. Lemon pasta is light creamy and easy to make. Just a few ingredients are all it takes to put together a refreshing simple meat.

LINGUINE WITH LEMON & TOMATOES

Serving size = 2; cook time = 35 minutes

Ingredients

1 c roasted tomatoes
4 very thin lemon slices
1 tbsp extra virgin olive oil
1 garlic clove, minced
1 tbsp lemon juice
6 oz linguine pasta
1 ½ c arugula
1 tbsp fresh thyme
3 oz fresh mozzarella, torn
¼ c toasted pine nuts
½ c fresh basil
Sea salt and freshly ground black pepper

Directions

Preheat the oven to 350 degrees F and line a small baking sheet with parchment paper. Place the lemon slices on the baking sheet. Drizzle with olive oil and sprinkle with salt. Roast for 15 to 20 minutes or until they're golden brown around the edges. Finely mince the lemons and set aside. In the bottom of a medium sized cold pot combine the olive oil, garlic, lemon juice and ¼ teaspoon sea salt.

Boil pasta for about 10 minutes. Reserve ¼ cup pasta water. Drain noodles and rinse with hot water. Scoop the hot pasta into the pot along with the reserved pasta water and the arugula. Toss. If necessary gently heat until the arugula wilts and the pasta is warmed through. Add the thyme, tomatoes and lemons and toss again. Top with the mozzarella, pine nuts and basil. Gently toss. Season to taste and serve.

Recipe notes: This simple recipe is flexible so feel free to play with it depending on your tastes and what's in your pantry.

SPAGHETTI BOLOGNESE

Serving size = 3-4; cook time = 35 minutes

Ingredients

2 tbsp olive oil
1 lrg onion finely chopped
1 lb ground beef
1 - 2 tbsp dried oregano
1 - 28 oz can of crushed or pureed tomatoes
3 cloves garlic chopped
2 tbsp tomato paste
1 good sized handful fresh parsley chopped
Salt and pepper to taste
½ lb spaghetti
Grated pecorino romano or parmesan cheese for serving optional

Directions

Heat the olive oil in a large pan over medium heat. Add the onions and sauté until lightly golden 2 to 3 minutes. Add the garlic and fry another minute. Add the ground beef; fry until fully cooked and no pink shows at all in the meat about 8 minutes. Add the oregano and tomato paste and mix with the meat. Add the tomatoes, parsley and bring to a boil. Season with the salt and pepper. Reduce the heat to low and cook for at least 15 minutes (you can cook longer for a deeper flavor). In the meantime boil pasta for about 10 minutes. Drain noodles and rinse with hot water. Serve topped with the sauce and cheese if using.

Recipe notes: Classic Italian meat sauce is a staple in most families. My super simple Spaghetti Bolognese is the perfect dinner for any night of the week and will wow your family or guests.

EASY ZITI BAKE

Serving size = 6-8; cook time = 1 hour 15 minutes

Ingredients

12 oz uncooked ziti or small tube pasta
2 lb ground beef
1 jar 24 oz spaghetti sauce
2 lrg eggs, beaten
1 carton 15 oz ricotta cheese
2 ½ c shredded mozzarella cheese, divided
½ c grated parmesan cheese

Directions

Boil pasta for about 10 minutes. Meanwhile preheat oven to 350 degrees. In a large skillet, cook beef over medium heat until no longer pink. Drain. Stir in spaghetti sauce. In a large bowl combine eggs, ricotta cheese, 1 ½ cups mozzarella cheese and the parmesan cheese. Drain noodles and rinse with hot water; add to cheese mixture and stir until blended. Spoon a third of the meat sauce into a greased 13 x 9 inch baking dish; top with half of the pasta mixture. Repeat layers. Top with remaining meat sauce. Cover and bake 40 minutes. Uncover; sprinkle with remaining mozzarella cheese. Bake 5 to 10 minutes longer or until cheese is melted. Let stand 15 minutes before serving.

Recipe notes: I enjoy making this baked ziti recipe for family and friends. It's easy to prepare and I like to get creative with the sauce. Sometimes I might add my home canned tomatoes, mushrooms or vegetables.

BAKED ZITI

Serving size = 8-10; cook time = 1 hour 15 minutes

Ingredients
12 oz uncooked ziti or small tube pasta
2 lb ground beef
1 jar (24 oz) spaghetti sauce
2 lrg eggs, beaten
1 crtn (15 oz) ricotta cheese
2 - ½ c shredded mozzarella cheese, divided
½ c grated Parmesan cheese

Directions
Boil pasta for about 10 minutes. Meanwhile preheat oven to 350 degrees. In a large skillet cook beef over medium heat until no longer pink. Drain. Stir in spaghetti sauce into skillet. In a large bowl, combine eggs, ricotta cheese, 2 2/3 cups mozzarella cheese and the Parmesan cheese. Drain noodles and rinse with hot water. Add pasta to cheese mixture and stir until blended. Spoon a third of the meat sauce into a greased 13x9 inch baking dish; top with half of the pasta mixture. Repeat layers. Top with remaining meat sauce.

Cover and bake 40 minutes. Uncover and sprinkle with remaining mozzarella cheese. Bake 5 to 10 minutes longer or until bubbly. Let stand 15 minutes before serving.

BUTTERNUT SQUASH STUFFED SHELLS WITH CREAM SAUCE

Serving size = 4; cook time = 1 hour 15 minutes

Ingredients

1 lrg butternut squash, roughly 2 lb
6 oz large pasta shells
2 tsp maple syrup
¼ tsp salt
1/8 tsp ground nutmeg
3 tbsp unsalted butter
1 c heavy cream
1 tsp garlic powder
1 tsp dried sage or 6 to 8 fresh leaves
1 tsp dried rosemary or 1 sprig fresh rosemary
¾ c grated parmesan (see note)
Fresh sage (for topping)

Directions

Preheat oven to 400 degrees. Slice butternut squash in half and scoop out seeds. Place each half cut side down in a large roasting dish and pour ½ inch of water into the bottom. Place in oven and bake until tender about 30 to 45 minutes. Once done remove and let cool. While squash is roasting boil pasta for about 10 minutes. Drain shells and rinse with hot water. Set aside.

When squash has cooled enough to handle scrape out the flesh into a bowl and discard the skins. Mix in maple syrup, salt and nutmeg until thoroughly incorporated. To make sauce melt butter in a medium sized pot over medium low heat. Pour in heavy cream, garlic, sage and rosemary. Reduce heat and continue to cook the sauce without boiling the cream until the cream has thickened slightly 3 to 4 minutes.

Gradually stir in ½ cup of parmesan and keep stirring until the cheese is completely melted. Pour ¼ of the sauce in the bottom of a medium baking dish. Spoon about 2 tablespoons of butternut filling into each pasta shell. Place stuffed pasta shell in the dish and repeat until pasta shells are filled. Pour remaining sauce over the shells and sprinkle with remaining ¼ cup of parmesan. Return stuffed shells in the oven and bake until it starts to bubble and slightly brown about 10 to 15 minutes. Serve with a sprinkle of fresh sage.

EASY ZUCCHINI LASAGNA

Serving size = 6; cook time = 55 minutes

Ingredients

4 med zucchini, sliced into ¼ inch slices
¼ c parmesan cheese
3 c mozzarella, shredded
3 c tomato sauce

Ricotta Filling

3 garlic cloves, minced
1 ½ c ricotta cheese
¼ c parmesan cheese
1 egg
Pinch of salt
¼ tsp black pepper
¼ c fresh basil, chopped (for dried basil use 2 tablespoon)

Directions

See ingredients for how to slice zucchini noodles. Preheat oven to 350 degrees. Lay zucchini noodles on paper towels and sprinkle with course sea salt. Let sit for 10 minutes so zucchini sweats any access moisture. Use paper towels to press and dry zucchini noodles. Mix all of ricotta filling ingredients together in bowl. In a 13 x 9 inch baking dish/pan layer lasagna –thin layer of sauce, zucchini noodles, ricotta filling and mozzarella cheese. Repeat until finished. On top layer with sauce, mozzarella cheese, and parmesan cheese. Bake for 40 minutes uncovered then broil for 1 to 2 minutes until cheese is browned. Sprinkle with chopped fresh basil. Slice and enjoy!

Directions

Boil pasta for about 10 minutes. Reserve 2 cups pasta water. Drain noodles and rinse with hot water. Transfer 1 cup pasta water to a large skillet. Bring to a gentle simmer then whisk in butter a piece at a time until melted. Whisking constantly gradually add cheese making sure it's completely melted and incorporated before adding more. Add pasta and toss to coat adding more pasta cooking liquid as needed until sauce blankets noodles completely. Serve topped with pepper and more cheese.

FETTUCINE ALFREDO

Serving size = 4-6; cook time = 15 minutes

Ingredients

12 oz fettucine
Kosher salt
¼ c (1/2 stick) unsalted butter
¾ c finely grated Parmesan,
plus more for serving
Freshly ground black pepper

VEGAN CREAMY TOMATO BASIL PASTA

Serving size = 6; cook time = 40 minutes

Ingredients

6 medium tomatoes, quartered
1 medium yellow onion, chopped
6 cloves garlic, peeled and smashed
¼ cup olive oil, separated
1 tsp salt, separated
¼ tsp pepper
1 lb of ziti pasta
1 c soaked cashews
Fresh basil, chopped, to taste

Directions

Preheat oven to 400 degrees and line a baking sheet with tin foil. Place tomatoes, onions, garlic, olive oil, ½ teaspoon salt and pepper onto baking sheet. Drizzle with 2 tablespoons olive oil. Toss making sure everything is coated. Roast at 400 degrees 20 minutes. While vegetables are roasting boil pasta for about 10 minutes. Drain noodles and rinse with hot water.

Remove baking sheet from oven and remove skin from tomatoes. Roast for an additional 10 minutes. Next transfer all ingredients on the baking sheet (including juices) into a blender along with soaked cashews and the remaining olive oil and salt. Blend until smooth. Taste and adjust salt as needed. Toss pasta with sauce and top with fresh basil and cracked pepper. Enjoy!

Recipe notes: Place cashews in a glass bowl and cover them with water. Cover with plastic wrap and let them soak overnight. Bring a small pot of water to a rolling boil. Add cashews to the pot and remove from the heat. Let the cashews sit for at least 15 minutes.

HOMEMADE MACARONI AND CHEESE

Serving size = 6; cook time = 1 hour

Ingredients

12 oz dry macaroni
¼ c butter
¼ c flour
1 ½ c milk
1 c light cream
½ tsp dry mustard powder
1 tsp onion powder
Salt & pepper to taste
1 can condensed cream of cheddar soup optional, 10.75oz
4 c sharp cheddar, divided
½ c fresh parmesan cheese

Directions

Preheat oven to 425 degrees. Boil pasta for about 10 minutes. Drain noodles and rinse with hot water. Melt butter over medium heat in a large saucepan. Whisk in flour and let cook 2 minutes while stirring. Slowly whisk in cream, milk, mustard powder, onion powder, salt and pepper to taste. Cook over medium heat while stirring until thickened. Remove from heat and stir in parmesan cheese & 3 cups cheddar cheese until melted. Add soup if using. Toss cheese sauce & macaroni noodles together. Pour into a greased 9 x 13 inch pan. Top with remaining cheese. Bake 18 to 24 minutes or until bubbly. Do not overcook. Cool 10 to 15 minutes before serving.

Recipe notes: This homemade mac and cheese casserole is the best you've ever had. Tender noodles in a velvety sauce for the perfectly irresistible dish!

pepper. Bring to boil and continue to boil 5 minutes or until most of the liquid evaporates. Remove from heat; stir in whipping cream and butter. Reduce heat and simmer 5 more minutes.

TOMATO-CREAM SAUCE FOR PASTA

Serving size = 5; cook time = 20 minutes

Ingredients

2 tbsp olive oil
1 onion, diced
1 clove garlic, minced
1 (14.5 oz) can Italian style diced tomatoes, undrained
1 tbsp dried basil leaves
¾ tsp white sugar
¼ tsp dried oregano
¼ tsp salt
1/8 tsp ground black pepper
½ c heavy cream
1 tbsp butter

Directions

In a saucepan sauté onion and garlic in olive oil over medium heat. Make sure it doesn't burn. Add tomatoes, basil, sugar, oregano, salt and

CREAMY PASTA POMODORO

Serving size = 4; cook time = 35 minutes

Ingredients

Basic marinara

1 tbsp extra – virgin olive oil
3 tbsp finely minced shallot
1 lrg garlic clove, finely minced
¼ tsp sea salt
Freshly ground black pepper
1 (14 oz) can chopped tomatoes
1 tsp balsamic vinegar
1/8 teaspoon cane sugar
Pinch of dried oregano
Pinch of crushed red pepper flakes

Creamy tomato sauce

Marinara recipe, from above
¼ c raw cashews (see note)
½ tbsp. tomato paste
¼ c water
¼ c pasta water
¼ to ½ tsp sea salt

For the pasta

10 oz rigatoni
Extra virgin olive oil for drizzling
2 med zucchini, sliced into thin half moons
2 tbsp fresh thyme leaves
2 (14 oz) cans Mutti Cherry Tomatoes, drained
6 c spinach or mix of spinach & arugula
¼ c chopped parsley or sliced basil
Sea salt and freshly ground black pepper

Directions

Make the marinara sauce: Heat the olive oil in a small pot over low heat. Add the shallots, garlic, salt and a few grinds of black pepper and cook for 3 minutes stirring often. Add the tomatoes and their juices, balsamic vinegar, can sugar, oregano and red pepper flakes. Cover and simmer over low heat for 15 minutes stirring occasionally. Make the creamy sauce: Add the marinara to a blender with the cashews, tomato paste, salt and ¼ cup of water. Blend until smooth. Set aside until ready to use.

Boil pasta for about 10 minutes. Reserve ¼ cup pasta water. Drain noodles and rinse with hot water. While the pasta cooks heat generous drizzles of olive oil in a nonstick skillet over medium heat. Add the zucchini, thyme and generous pinches of salt and pepper. Sauté stirring occasionally until lightly browned about 3 minutes. Stir in ¼ cup hot pasta cooking water to loosen it up so that it will nicely coat the pasta.

Add the tomatoes and reduce the heat to low. Cook for 2 to 3 more minutes or until heated through. Add the spinach and gently toss until wilted. Season to taste with more salt and pepper. Scoop the pasta into individual bowls and add scoops of the creamy sauce. Toss to coat. Distribute the vegetables among the bowls and top with parsley and or basil. Season to taste and serve.

Recipe notes: if you're not using a high powered blender such as a Vitamix soak the cashews for 2 plus hours to make a creamier sauce. Drain before adding to the recipe.

CREAMY SWEET CORN PASTA

Serving size = 4; cook time = 20 minutes

Ingredients
5 ears corn
2 tbsp extra virgin olive oil
½ c chopped yellow onion
2 garlic cloves, crushed
½ c raw cashews
¼ c water, plus more if necessary
2 tablespoons fresh lemon juice
¼ tsp smoked paprika
½ tsp sea salt plus more to taste
Freshly ground black pepper
9 oz wide noodle pasta
2 scallions, finely sliced
3 packed cups fresh spinach
½ c sliced fresh basil, for serving (optional)
Microgreens, for serving (optional)

Directions
Slice the kernels off the corn cobbs then use the back of a chef's knife to scrape the milky liquid that's left on the cob. Heat 1 tablespoon of the olive oil in a medium skillet over medium heat. Add the onion and cook until soft about 3 minutes. Add 1 ½ cups of the corn and the whole crushed garlic cloves and cook until tender about 3 minutes more. Transfer to a blender and add the milky corn liquid, cashews, water, lemon juice, smoked paprika, salt and a few grinds of black pepper. Blend until creamy adding more water as needed to create a pourable consistency. Set aside.

Boil pasta for about 10 minutes. Reserve ¾ cup of pasta water. Drain noodles and rinse with hot water. Meanwhile wipe out the skillet and heat the remaining 1 tablespoon olive oil over medium heat. Add the remaining corn, scallions, a pinch of salt and a few grinds of black pepper and cook stirring occasionally until tender about 3 minutes. Add the spinach, cooked pasta, the corn sauce and ½ to ¾ cup of the reserved pasta water as needed to create a creamy sauce. Season to taste and serve immediately with the sliced basil and microgreens if using.

Recipe notes: Vegan - use eggless pasta. Gluten Free - use gluten free pasta.

CREAMY PASTA BAKE WITH BRUSSEL SPROUTS

Serving size = 4-6; cook time = 35 minutes

Ingredients

White miso sauce

1 c raw slivered almonds
2 tbsp white miso paste
2 garlic cloves
½ tsp Dijon mustard
1 c Almond Breeze almond milk original sweetened
¼ c fresh lemon juice
2 tbsp extra virgin olive oil
½ tsp sea salt

For the pasta

10 oz shell pasta
1 tbsp extra virgin olive oil
3 c Brussel sprouts, slice in half
2 tbsp white wine, or water, to deglaze the pan
2 scallions, sliced
Sea salt and freshly ground black pepper

Bread crumb topping

1 tbsp panko bread crumbs
1 tbsp hemp seeds
1/8 tsp sea salt
Extra virgin olive oil, for drizzling
¼ c chopped fresh herbs (chives, tarragon, or parsley

Directions

Preheat the oven to 400 degrees and brush a 7 x 9 inch or similar size baking dish with olive oil. Make the white miso sauce: In a high speed blender combine the almonds, miso paste, garlic, Dijon mustard, almond milk, lemon juice, olive oil and salt and blend until smooth.

Make the pasta: Boil pasta for about 10 minutes. Drain noodles and rinse with hot water. Heat the 1 tablespoon olive oil in a medium skillet over medium high heat. Add the brussels sprouts and cook stirring occasionally until browned and tender 6 to 8 minutes. Remove from the heat and add the wine and stir to scrape up any bits that have stuck to the bottom of the pan. Add the cooked pasta, the scallions with the miso sauce to the pan. Stir to coat then transfer to the baking dish. Top with the panko bread crumbs, hemp seeds, a few pinches of salt and cheese if using. Drizzle the top with olive oil.

Bake covered for 15 minutes or until the brussel sprouts are fully tender and the dish is just warmed through. This short cooking time will prevent the filling from drying out. Remove from the oven and sprinkle with the fresh herbs and serve.

Recipe notes: If you're not vegan and want to bake this with cheese on top, sprinkle 1 ½ cups shredded mozzarella cheese and bake uncovered until bubbly for 20 to 25 minutes.

ROASTED VEGETABLE PASTA

Serving size = 4-6; cook time = 1 hour

Ingredients

4 carrots, cut into 1 inch pieces
2 Vidalia onions, or 1 small yellow onion, cut into 1 inch pieces
5 small patty pan squash, sliced in halt
2 small zucchini, cut into 1 inch pieces
10 cherry tomatoes
1 tablespoon extra-virgin olive oil, more for drizzling
1 tablespoon sherry vinegar
2 garlic cloves, minced
½ teaspoon herbs de Provence
Leaves from 8 sprigs fresh thyme, more for garnish
1 (16 oz) package penne pasta
½ c crumbled feta cheese
½ c fresh basil, more for garnish
Juice of ½ small lemon, more if desired
Pinches of red pepper flakes
Sea salt and freshly ground black pepper

Directions

Preheat the oven to 400 degrees and line 2 large baking sheets with parchment paper. Place the carrots and onions on the first sheet and the patty pan squash, zucchini, and tomatoes on the other. Drizzle both sheets of vegetables with olive oil and generous pinches of salt and pepper. Place the sheet with the carrots and onions in the oven first and roast for 30 to 35 minutes or until the onions are tender and lightly charred and the carrots are tender and browned. Place the second sheet in and roast for 20 minutes or until the squash and zucchini are golden brown around the edges and the tomatoes are lightly bursting. Remove from the oven and set aside. In the bottom of a large bowl combine the 1 tablespoon of olive oil with the sherry vinegar, garlic, herbs de Provence, thyme, ¼ teaspoon salt and several grinds of black pepper. Stir in the roasted vegetables.

Boil pasta for about 10 minutes. Drain noodles and rinse with hot water. Transfer the cooked pasta to the large bowl with the roasted vegetables and toss to coat. Add the feta, basil, lemon juice and red pepper flakes and gently toss. Season (generously) to taste with more salt, pepper and lemon juice as desired. Garnish with more fresh herbs and a generous drizzle of olive oil.

SUN DRIED TOMATO PASTA WITH KALE

Serving size = 4; cook time = 15 minutes

Ingredients

½ cup olive oil
1 bunch Tuscan kale ribs removed and roughly chopped
8 cloves, garlic finely minced
1 tsp red pepper flakes
1 lemon zested and juiced
1/ c sun dried tomatoes the kind in oil, roughly chopped
¾ c white wine
10 oz spaghetti
¾ c shredded mozzarella
Kosher salt and freshly cracked black pepper to taste

Directions

Heat the olive oil over medium heat in a skillet. Once hot add the kale, red pepper flakes and season with salt and pepper and cook until wilted. Add the garlic and sauté for 30 seconds until fragrant. Add the sun dried tomatoes, lemon zest and stir to combine. Add the white wine and cook until alcohol cooks off. Remove from the heat and stir in the lemon juice. Stir to combine and taste. Adjust seasoning as needed. Boil pasta for about 10 minutes. Reserve ½ cup pasta water. Drain noodles and rinse with hot water. In a bowl toss with sauce, reserved water, cheese and season with salt and pepper as needed. Serve immediately.

Recipe notes: Sun Dried Tomato and Kale Pasta with a white wine sauce is my new go to panty staple meal. It's meant to serve 4 but Richard and I devoured it just the 2 of us. It's that good!

HERB AND GARLIC MUSHROOM PASTA

Serving size = 4-6; cook time = 25 minutes

Ingredients

2 tbsp extra virgin olive oil
16 oz cremini mushrooms, de-stemmed and sliced
8 oz spaghetti, plus 1/3 cup reserved pasta water
2 garlic cloves, minced
¼ c dry white wine (such as chardonnay or pinot grigio)
¼ to 1/3 c cashew cream (below)
1/3 c chopped fresh tarragon
1/3 c chopped fresh chives
1/3 c shaved Parmigiano Reggiano cheese
Sea salt and freshly ground black pepper
Savory cashew cream (this makes extra)*
1/3 c raw cashews + ½ cup water (or skip this mixture and use regular cream)
½ clove garlic (a medium one)
½ tsp fresh lemon juice
½ tsp Dijon mustard
Salt to taste

Directions

Make the cashew cream by blending all ingredients in a high speed blender until smooth. Set aside. (Note: it's not going to be very thick, it should be the consistency of half & half or heavy cream). In a large pan heat the olive oil over medium heat. Add the mushrooms, a few generous pinches of salt and pepper and cook until soft and wilted stirring occasionally about 8 to 12 minutes. Meanwhile boil pasta for about 10 minutes. Reserve 1/3 cup pasta water. Drain noodles and rinse with hot water.

To the mushrooms add the wine. Stir and let it reduce for 1 to 2 minutes. Stir in the garlic and the cooked pasta and toss. Add a few splashes of the cashew cream and a few splashes of the pasta water and toss to create a light sauce. Add half of the fresh herbs and season to taste. Serve immediately with remaining fresh herbs and Parmigiano Reggiano cheese on top.

Recipe notes: To make this vegan skip the cheese and serve with a few drizzles of balsamic vinegar. Change up the herbs: Rosemary and/or sage would be delicious here but add those heartier herbs to the pan as you add the mushrooms so that they'll cook more than the softer herbs.

ONE POT PENNE PASTA

Serving size= 6-8; cook time = 15 minutes

Ingredients

6 oz penne pasta
1 ½ c sliced cherry tomatoes
1 ½ c thinly sliced leeks
1 c zucchini, sliced into ¼ inch thick half moons
½ c thinly sliced red bell pepper
3 sm garlic cloves, minced
2 tbsp extra virgin olive oil
2 tbsp lemon juice, plus 1 tsp zest
1 tsp dried oregano
1 tsp sea salt
½ tsp red pepper flakes
1 sprig of basil
2 ¼ c water

Top with chopped parsley, toasted pine nuts and grated parmesan cheese or Vegan Hemp Seed Topping optional.

Vegan Hemp Seed Topping

½ c hemp seeds
2 tbsp nutritional yeast
2 tbsp raw sunflower seeds
Pinch of sea salt

Directions

In a large pot, combine the pasta, tomatoes, leeks, zucchini, bell pepper, garlic, olive oil, lemon juice and zest, oregano, salt, red pepper flakes and basil. Add the water and stir. Bring to a boil cover and boil for 8 minutes. Give it a stir around the 5 minute mark to make sure nothing is sticking to the bottom of the pan and put the cover back on. At 8 minutes test the pasta for doneness. Remove the pot from the heat stir and let it sit for about 2 minutes to allow the sauce to thicken.

Make the Vegan Hemp Seed Topping: In a food processor combine the hemp seeds, nutritional yeast, sunflower seeds and salt and pulse to combine. Serve with the chopped parsley, toasted pine nuts and parmesan cheese or vegan hemp seed topping if using.

RIGATONI WITH CHICKEN AND BROCCOLI BOLOGNESE

Serving size = 4; cook time = 25 minutes

Ingredients

12 oz rigatoni
1 tbsp olive oil
2 cloves garlic, pressed
1 lb ground chicken breast
½ tsp red pepper flakes
Kosher salt and pepper
½ c dry white wine
1 c low sodium chicken broth
½ lb broccoli crowns, finely chopped
1 tbsp finely grated lemon zest
½ c finely grated Parmesan, plus more for serving
¼ c flat leaf parsley, chopped
1 tbsp tarragon, chopped
2 tbsp chopped chives
2 tbsp cold unsalted butter (optional)

Directions

Boil pasta for about 10 minutes. Reserve 1 cup pasta water. Drain noodles and rinse with hot water. Meanwhile heat oil in a large skillet on medium. Add garlic and cook stirring until it starts to sizzle about 1 minute; add chicken. Season with red pepper flakes and ½ tsp each salt and pepper and cook breaking it up into very tiny pieces with a spoon until just cooked through about 6 minutes. Add wine and simmer until nearly evaporated about 2 minutes.
Add broth and then broccoli and toss to combine then bring to a simmer. Cover and simmer until broccoli is just tender 5 to 6 minutes. Fold in lemon zest, parmesan and herbs. Remove from heat and add butter if using stirring and tossing until melted. Toss with rigatoni adding some reserved pasta water if pasta seems dry. Top with additional Parmesan if desired.

BROKEN LASAGNA WITH WALNUT PESTO

Serving size = 6; cook time = 20 minutes

Ingredients

1 c walnut halves (4 ounces)
2 c lightly packed basil leaves
1 lrg garlic clove, thinly sliced
¼ c extra virgin olive oil
¾ c freshly grated Parmigiano-Reggiano cheese
Salt and freshly ground pepper
1 lb whole wheat lasagna noodles, broken into 1 inch pieces
6 oz watercress, arugula or other bitter greens, thick stems discarded and leaves coarsely chopped
Sautéed mushrooms, for serving

Directions

Preheat the oven to 350 degrees. Spread the walnuts on a baking sheet and toast for 8 to 10 minutes, until they are fragrant and lightly browned. Let cool completely. Coarsely chop half of the walnuts and set the remaining toasted walnuts aside.

In a food processor pulse the remaining walnuts with the basil and garlic until the walnuts are finely chopped. With the machine on add the olive oil in a thin stream and process until the pesto is almost smooth. Add ½ cup of the cheese and pulse until just incorporated. Transfer the walnut pesto to a bowl and season it with salt and pepper.

Boil pasta for about 10 minutes. Reserve ½ cup pasta water. Drain noodles and rinse with hot water. Return to pot. Add the watercress and walnut pesto and toss well. Add the reserved pasta water and toss again until well coated. Transfer the pasta to bowls and garnish with the remaining ¼ cup of cheese, the chopped walnuts and sautéed mushrooms. Serve.

Recipe notes: Whole grain pasta is one of the easiest ways to sneak whole grains into your diet. Made with noodles broken into 1 inch pieces features a healthy pesto made with walnuts and basil.

EGG NOODLES WITH CRAB, SNAP PEAS, ORANGE AND CHILES

Serving size = 4; cook time = 15 minutes

Ingredients
12 oz wide egg noodles
2 tbsp cold unsalted butter
1 tbsp finely grated orange zest
¼ c fresh orange juice
1 tbsp olive oil
8 oz sugar snap peas, halved on a diagonal
2 red chilies, thinly sliced
1 tbsp fresh lemon juice
2 6 oz cans crab meat, drained and picked over
¼ c basil leaves

Directions
Boil pasta for about 10 minutes. Drain noodles and rinse with hot water. In the same pot toss with butter, orange zest and orange juice. Meanwhile heat oil in a large skillet on medium high. Cook snap peas for 2 minutes until lightly browned. Add chilies and cook 1 minute. Remove from heat and toss with pasta, lemon juice, crab and basil. Serve right away.
Recipe notes: This 15 minute dinner is the perfect pasta dish to make for a sophisticated dinner party and no one will know it's so easy.

BUTTERNUT SQUASH SPAGHETTI WITH SAUSAGE AND SAGE

Serving size = 4; cook time = 40 minutes

Ingredients

3 c butternut squash, cut into ¼" dice
3 tbsp unsalted butter, divided
½ lb sweet italian pork sausage
8 fresh sage leaves
8 oz pasta, cooked al dente
¾ c heavy cream
1 tbsp sherry vinegar
¼ c grated parmesan cheese

Directions

Heat 2 tablespoons butter in a large skillet over medium high heat until hot and the butter starts to brown. Add the diced butternut squash and 4 sage leaves. Cook for about 10 to 12 minutes until brown and tender stirring frequently. Season with kosher salt & freshly ground pepper. Remove the squash from the skillet and set aside. Remove the sausage from its casing and add to the skillet with a little oil breaking it up into bite size pieces with the back of a spoon or spatula. Brown and cook through.

Add the squash back to the skillet along with 4 more sage leaves and 1 tablespoon butter. Cook for another 2 minutes to crisp sage leaves. Reduce the heat to low and add heavy cream cooking for about 2 minutes until the sauce thickens. Add the cooked pasta, vinegar and grated parmesan cheese. Gently stir to combine and remove from heat. If the sauce is too thick add a little reserved pasta water. Serve immediately with more grated parmesan.

LEMON BROCCOLI PESTO PASTA

Serving size = 6; cook time = 30 minutes

Ingredients

Kosher salt
12 oz frozen broccoli (or 1 head broccoli, stems and florets)
6 tbsp pine nuts, lightly toasted
3 c grated parmesan cheese
2 c packed fresh basil leaves, plus more for garnish
Zest and juice of 2 lemons, plus more for serving
1 c extra virgin olive oil
Freshly cracked black pepper
1 lb short pasta like rotini (use whole wheat pasta for Mediterranean diet option)

Directions

Bring a large pot of water to a boil. Salt generously. Add the broccoli and cook until crisp tender (about 3 to 4 minutes). Use a slotted spoon to transfer the broccoli to a large bowl of ice water. Do not discard the cooking water (you will use it to cook the pasta later). Drain the broccoli and dry on a paper towel.

In the bowl of a food processor combine the broccoli, 4 tablespoon of the pine nuts, 1 ½ cups of parmesan, the basil leaves and lemon zest and juice. Process until combined (about 30 seconds or so). Scrape down the sides of the bowl cover and run the processor again. And while the processor is running slowly steam in the extra virgin olive oil. Season with salt and pepper to taste.

Boil pasta for about 10 minutes. Reserve ¼ cup pasta water. Drain noodles and rinse with hot water. Return the drained pasta to the pot over medium low heat. Add 1 cup of the Parmesan cheese and the reserved ¼ cup of pasta water and cook stirring constantly until the cheese coats the pasta (about 1 minute).

Remove from the heat and add half of the broccoli pesto (I added a bit more than half). Toss to coat the pasta with the broccoli pesto. (Reserve extra broccoli pesto or freeze it for a later use). Transfer the pasta to a large serving bowl. Top with the remaining Parmesan cheese, 2 tablespoons pine nuts and a little lemon zest. Garnish with a few basil leaves. Enjoy!

Recipe notes: You will use only about ½ or a little more of the broccoli pesto. Transfer the rest to an air tight freezer safe container or jar and freeze for later use.

Pine nut replacement: Pine nuts are your best bet for pesto, but they can be pricey and less available than other nuts. If you must replace pine nuts try shelled walnuts (walnut hearts).

SESAME-GARLIC BEEF & BROCCOLI WITH WHOLE WHEAT NOODLES

Serving size = 4; cook time = 1 hour

Ingredients

1 lb boneless beef sirloin steak, trimmed
2 tbsp reduced sodium soy sauce
2 tbsp lemon juice
1 tbsp toasted sesame oil, plus
2 teaspoons, divided
3 cloves garlic, minced
1 tsp all spice
¼ tsp crushed red pepper
6 oz whole wheat linguine
4 c broccoli florets
½ c water
½ c slivered onion
1/8 tsp ground pepper
1 tsp toasted sesame seeds
4 wedges Lemon wedges for serving

Directions

Thinly slice beef across the grain into bite size strips. Place in a resalable plastic bag and set in a shallow dish. Combine soy sauce, lemon juice, 1 tablespoon sesame oil, garlic, ginger and crushed red pepper in a small bowl; pour over the beef. Seal the bag; turn to coat. Refrigerate for 30 minutes turning the bag once.

Boil pasta for about 10 minutes. Reserve ½ cup pasta water. Drain noodles and rinse with hot water. Meanwhile combine broccoli and water in a wok or medium nonstick skillet; bring to a boil over medium high heat. Cook until the water is evaporated 3 to 4 minutes. Add onion, pepper and the remaining 2 teaspoon sesame oil. Cook stirring occasionally until the broccoli is crisp tender 3 to 4 minutes. Transfer the broccoli mixture to a bowl and cover and keep warm.

Drain the beef reserving the marinade. Add half of the beef to the hot wok (or skillet); cook, stirring, until slightly pink in the center 3 to 5 minutes. Transfer to a plate and keep warm. Repeat with the remaining beef; remove to the plate.

Combine the reserved cooking water and marinade in the wok (or skillet); add the noodles. Cook over medium heat stirring just until the noodles are tender and the sauce is thickened slightly 2 to 3 minutes. Divide the noodle mixture among 4 plates or shallow bowls. Top with the beef and the broccoli mixture. Sprinkle with sesame seeds and serve with lemon wedges if desired.

PASTA SALADS

TOMATO MOZZARELLA PASTA SALAD WITH BALSAMIC VINEGARETTE

Serving size = 6; cook time = 25 minutes

Ingredients

8 oz rotini
Salt for pasta water
3 c fresh spinach
1 pt grape tomatoes
8 oz mozzarella

Parmesan Balsamic Vinaigrette

1/3 c olive oil
3 tbsp balsamic vinegar
2 tbsp mayonnaise
2 tbsp grated Parmesan
½ tbsp Dijon mustard
1 clove garlic, minced
½ tsp dried basil
¼ tsp salt
Freshly cracked pepper

Directions

Boil pasta for about 10 minutes. Drain noodles and rinse with cold water. Combine all the dressings' ingredients in a jar or blender. Either blend until combined or shake your jar until the ingredients are well combined. Set the dressing aside until needed. Roughly chop the spinach and slice the grape tomatoes in half. Dice the mozzarella into ½ inch cubes.

Add the spinach, tomatoes and mozzarella to a large bowl. Once the pasta is well drained and mostly cooked add it to the bowl with the mozzarella and vegetables. Make sure the pasta is no longer hot so it doesn't wilt the spinach or melt the cheese. Toss the ingredients to combine. If serving the salad later store it like this without dressing. If serving immediately add half of the dressing and toss to coat. Add more dressing as desired.

Recipe notes: This Tomato Mozzarella Pasta Salad with homemade parmesan balsamic vinaigrette is the perfect light and fresh summer meal. Perfect for potlucks. Fresh mozzarella is best but block or stick mozzarella can be used in its place. Whole milk mozzarella (not part-skim) if possible.

GREENS PASTA SALAD

Serving size = 4-6; cook time = 45 minutes

Ingredients

Ice
Kosher salt
Pepper
1 lb asparagus, trimmed and cut into 1-inch lengths
2 c peas, fresh or frozen
1 lb campanelle pasta
1 c buttermilk
½ c mayonnaise
3 tbsp Champagne vinegar
1 lrg garlic clove, grated
½ lb arugula (not baby), thick stems discarded, leaves coarsely chopped

Directions

Set up an ice bath. In a large saucepan of salted boiling water cook the asparagus and peas until crisp tender about 2 minutes. Drain and transfer the vegetables to the ice bath to cool completely; drain well. Boil pasta for about 10 minutes. Drain noodles and rinse with cold water. Transfer to a large bowl. Whisk in the buttermilk with the mayonnaise, vinegar and garlic. Season with salt and pepper. Toss half of the dressing with the warm pasta; let cool for 30 minutes. Stir in the asparagus, peas and remaining dressing. Season with salt and pepper then fold in the arugula and serve.

Recipe notes: The pasta salad can be refrigerated for a few hours. Fold in the arugula before serving.

QUICK AND EASY PASTA SALAD

Serving size = 8-10; cook time = 20 minutes

Ingredients
Pasta Salad
1 lb dried fusilli pasta
1 c sliced bell pepper (1 medium)
1 c thinly sliced zucchini (1/2 medium)
1 c halved cherry tomatoes
1/3 c thinly sliced scallions (5 to 6)
¼ c sliced pepperoncini or banana peppers, optional
1 c (4 oz) halved mixed olives
1 c (2 oz) grated parmesan cheese or hard cheese
1 c (6 oz) fresh mozzarella balls, chopped
1/3 c fresh parsley or basil, optional

Homemade Dressing
1/3 c red wine vinegar, white wine vinegar or champagne vinegar
½ tsp fine sea salt, plus more to taste
½ tsp fresh ground black pepper
½ tsp dried oregano
2 to 3 tbsp juice from pepperoncini jar, optional
½ c extra virgin olive oil

Directions
Boil pasta for about 10 minutes. Drain noodles and rinse with cold water. In the bottom of a large bowl make the dressing. Whisk the red wine vinegar, salt, pepper, oregano, pepperoncini juice (if using) and the olive oil until blended. Add the drained and rinsed pasta to the dressing and mix well. Stir in the bell pepper, zucchini, tomatoes, scallions, pepperoncini (if using), olives, parmesan, mozzarella, and the herbs (if using). Taste for seasoning and adjust with salt and pepper as needed. Serve or for the best results cover and refrigerate at least 30 minutes and up to 5 days.

Recipe notes: This gets better and better over time so making it a day in advance is a great idea.

VINEGAR-GLAZED BUTTERNUT SQUASH PASTA SALAD

Serving size = 4; cook time = 40 minutes

Ingredients

1 (2 lb) butternut squash – peeled, seeded and cut into ¾ inch pieces (6 cups)
¼ c plus 2 tbsp red wine vinegar
2 tbsp extra virgin olive oil
1 tbsp honey
Kosher salt
Pepper
¾ lb fusilli pasta
¼ c plus 1 tablespoon refined hazelnut oil
1 heat of Treviso or ½ a small head of radicchio, thinly sliced
½ c packed parsley leaves
Shaved Pecorino Toscano or Romano, for serving

Directions

Preheat the oven to 425 degrees. On a rimmed baking sheet toss the squash with ¼ cup of the vinegar, the olive and honey and spread evenly on the baking sheet. Season with salt and pepper. Roast for about 35 minutes tossing halfway through until browned and glazed. Boil pasta for about 10 minutes. Drain noodles and rinse with cold water.

In a large bowl whisk the remaining 2 tablespoons each of vinegar and hazelnut oil. Stir in the squash, treviso and parsley then fold in the pasta. Season with salt and pepper. Serve warm or at room temperature with shaved pecorino.

Recipe notes: The pasta salad can be refrigerated overnight. Stir in the Treviso and parsley before serving.

PASTA WITH TOFU AND CUCUMBER

Serving size = 4; cook time = 30 minutes

Ingredients

¾ lb spaghetti
1 ¼ lb firm tofu
1 tbsp plus 4 teaspoon soy sauce
2 ½ tsp grated fresh ginger
2 ½ tbsp. cooking oil
2 tbsp wine vinegar
1 ½ tsp lemon juice
1 tsp Asian sesame oil
¾ tsp grated lemon zest
¼ tsp salt
1 tsp cayenne pepper
2 cucumbers
3 scallions including green tops
3 tbsp chopped cilantro or fresh parsley

Directions

Boil pasta for about 10 minutes. Drain noodles and rinse with cold water. In a medium bowl combine the tofu with the 1 tablespoon soy sauce and ½ teaspoon of the grated ginger. Let sit for about 5 minutes. In a large glass or stainless steel bowl combine the remaining 2 teaspoons ginger and 4 teaspoons soy sauce, 1 ½ tablespoons of the cooking oil, the vinegar, lemon juice, sesame oil, lemon zest, salt and cayenne.

In a large nonstick frying pan heat the remaining 1 tablespoon cooking oil over moderate heat. Add the tofu and cook stirring frequently until browned about 8 minutes. Add the tofu, pasta, cucumbers, scallions and cilantro to the dressing in the large bowl and toss.

Suggested pairing: The crisp citrus tang of a German Riesling Spatlese Halbtrocken is just right for this summery dish and its Asian flavors. Halbtrocken means half dry or just a little sweet. Try one from the Pfalz where the sunny climate yields fruity wines.

PASTA SALAD WITH GRILLED SAUSAGE AND PEPPERS

Serving size = 6-8; cook time = 45 minutes

Ingredients

1 lb gemelli pasta
6 tbsp extra virgin olive oil
3 tbsp freshly squeezed lemon juice
1 ½ tsp finely grated lemon zest
1 tbsp tomato paste
2 lrg garlic cloves
1 lrg shallot
1 ½ tsp chopped thyme
Salt
Freshly ground black pepper
Sausage Mixed Grill (sausages and vegetables thinly sliced)
2 lrg celery ribs
¼ lb smoked mozzarella
1 c chopped basil

Directions

Boil pasta for about 10 minutes. Reserve ¼ cup of pasta water. Drain noodles and rinse with cold water. Transfer the pasta to a large bowl. Drizzle lightly with olive oil and toss to coat. Let cool to room temperature. Meanwhile in a medium bowl stir the lemon juice with the lemon zest, tomato paste, garlic, shallot and thyme. Stir in the 6 tablespoons of olive oil and the reserved pasta cooking water.

Season the dressing with salt and pepper. Add ¼ cup of the dressing to the pasta and toss. Add sausages, peppers, radicchio (from the Sausage Mixed Grill recipe), celery, mozzarella and the remaining dressing and toss well. Season the pasta salad with salt and pepper. Sprinkle with the basil and serve.

RICE NOODLE SALAD WITH CHICKEN AND HERBS

Serving size = 4-6; cook time = 40 minutes

Ingredients
½ lb dried rice noodles
¾ c fresh grapefruit juice
2 lrg garlic cloves, minced
2 tbsp sugar
¼ c plus 1 tablespoon Asian fish sauce
½ lb cabbage, finely shredded (4 cups)
3 lrg scallions, thinly sliced
½ lb cooked chicken, cut into long strips
½ c chopped cilantro
¼ c chopped mint
Sriracha for serving

In a bowl cover the noodles with cold water and let stand until pliable for 25 minutes. Drain. Bring a saucepan of water to a boil. Add the noodles and cook stirring until al dente 1 minute. Drain the noodles in a colander and return them to the pan. Fill the saucepan with cold water and swish the noodles around. Drain and whisk the noodles 2 more times.

Drain the noodles in the colander lifting and tossing until dry. In a small bowl stir the grapefruit juice with the garlic, sugar and fish sauce until the sugar is dissolved. In a large bowl toss the rice noodles with the shredded cabbage and scallions. Add the dressing and toss well. Add the chicken, cilantro and mint and toss. Serve right away passing Sriracha sauce at the table.

Recipe notes: The dressing can be refrigerated overnight.

GRILLED SUMMER VEGETABLE PASTA SALAD

Serving size = 4-5; cook time = 1 hour 30 minutes

Ingredients

1 lb rotini pasta
2 med zucchini squash
2 med yellow squash
2 ears corn
½ red onion
1 lb asparagus
2 bell peppers, sliced thick, I use an assortment of colors.
Olive oil to brush on veggies
4 tbsp olive oil
4 tbsp Dijon mustard
4 tbsp red wine vinegar, I use 2
1 lemon, juiced
2 tsp basil, dried
2 tsp parsley, dried
2 tsp oregano, dried
Salt and pepper to taste
2 to 4 oz feta cheese
½ pt grape tomatoes, sliced in half

Directions

Boil pasta for about 10 minutes. Drain noodles and rinse with hot water. Mix dressing ingredients together in a measuring bowl. Slice squash and onion into halves or large slices. Slice bell pepper into thick ringed slices. Leave corn and asparagus whole. Brush on or drizzle with olive oil and sprinkle with salt to taste. Set outdoor grill to high heat or cast iron grill over medium high heat. Grill until al dente or desired doneness. Remove and slice into bite sized chunks. Run knife down corn to remove kernels. In a large bowl toss pasta, vegetables and dressing together. Top with feta cheese and tomatoes. Serve immediately warm or cover and refrigerate until serving.

Recipe notes: Grilled summer vegetable pasta salad is a mixture of delicious pasta mixed with the cream of the summer crops veggies. These crisp grilled vegetables along with rotini pasta are tossed in a light dressing and loaded with beautiful color and flavor. As it sits in the refrigerator the flavors intensify. I typically make this the morning I am serving and let it sit in the refrigerator for a few hours to overnight.

BOW-TIE SALAD WITH FENNEL, PROSCIUTTO AND PARMESAN

Serving size = 4; cook time = 15 minutes

Ingredients

½ lb bow tie pasta
1 lrg fennel bulb (about 1 pound), sliced as thin as possible
¼ c olive oil
2 tbsp lemon juice
¼ tsp salt
½ tsp fresh ground black pepper
¼ lb thin-sliced prosciutto, cut into strips
¼ lb chunk Parmesan cheese or 1/3 cup grated Parmesan

Directions

Boil pasta for about 10 minutes. Drain noodles and rinse with cold water. In a large bowl toss together the bow ties, fennel, oil, lemon juice, salt and ¼ teaspoon of the pepper. Add the prosciutto and toss again. To serve mound the salad on plates. Top with strips of Parmesan shaved from the chunk of cheese with a vegetable peeler or with the grated Parmesan. Sprinkle the remaining ¼ teaspoon pepper over the cheese.

Recipe notes: The easiest way to slice fennel is to cut off the stalks, cut the bulb in half from the top through the root end, lay each half flat side down and slice. For that matter this is a good technique for almost any round fruit or vegetable.

Suggested pairing: Have some fun with this dish and try a bottle of the sparkling Italian wine Prosecco. It should go nicely with the fennel.

NICOISE-STYLE ORZO SALAD

Serving size = 4; cook time = 15 minutes

Ingredients

½ lb orzo
½ c Nicoise olives, pitted
½ c pear or cherry tomatoes
½ sm red onion, finely chopped
¼ c finely chopped flat leaf parsley
1 ½ tbsp. drained capers
1 tbsp balsamic vinegar
1 garlic clove, minced
Kosher salt and freshly ground pepper
¼ c extra virgin olive oil

Directions

Boil pasta for about 10 minutes. Drain and rinse with cold water. Transfer the orzo to a bowl and add the olives, tomatoes, onion, parsley and capers. In a small bowl combine the vinegar, garlic and a pinch of kosher salt and pepper. Whisk in the olive oil and stir the dressing into the pasta salad.

FARFALLE WITH SPRING VEGEGABLES

Serving size = 4-6; cook time = 40 minutes

Ingredients

2 slices white sandwich bread
(1 cup finely chopped)
½ c plus 2 tablespoon extra-virgin olive oil
2 tablespoon chopped flat leaf parsley
2 tablespoon snipped chives
1 tablespoon chopped tarragon
Salt and freshly ground pepper
1 bunch broccolini
1 lb farfalle
4 tbsp unsalted butter
1 garlic clove (minced)
1 fennel bulb (halved, cored and thinly sliced)
2 scallions (thinly sliced)
1 c frozen peas, thawed or pound
fresh peas, shelled
1 tbsp fresh lemon juice

Directions

Preheat the oven to 350 degrees. On a baking sheet toss the bread with ¼ cup of the oil and toast for 8 to 10 minutes stirring once until golden. Let cool then stir in half each of the parsley, chives and tarragon. Season the crumbs with salt and pepper. In a pot of boiling salted water cook the broccolini until tender; 1 minute using tongs and transfer to a cutting board and coarsely chop. Boil pasta for about 10 minutes. Reserve 1 cup pasta water. Drain noodles and rinse with cold water.

In a deep skillet melt the butter in the remaining 6 tablespoons of oil. Add garlic, fennel, scallions, peas and broccolini and cook over moderate heat until the fennel is crisp tender about 6 minutes. Add the pasta, lemon juice and cooking water and season with salt and pepper. Cook over moderate heat until the water is nearly absorbed. Stir in the remaining herbs. Sprinkle the pasta with the bread crumbs just before serving.

Recipe notes: The pasta can be kept at room temperature for 4 hours. The crumbs can be stored at room temperature overnight.

Suggested pairing: Zesty, herbal Sauvignon Blanc.

PAELLA SALAD

Serving size = 6-8; cook time = 30 minutes

Ingredients

2 ½ tbsp olive oil
1 onion, chopped
1 green bell pepper, chopped
1 ¼ tsp salt
6 oz dried chorizo or other firm spicy sausage such as pepperoni, quartered lengthwise and sliced thin crosswise
¼ tsp paprika
1 lb boneless, skinless chicken breasts (about 3), cut into ½ inch cubes
¼ tsp fresh ground black pepper
½ lb orzo (about 1 cup)
2 tbsp lemon juice
1 tomato, diced
½ c chopped fresh parsley

Directions

In a large frying pan heat 1 ½ tablespoons of the oil over moderately low heat. Add the onion, bell pepper and ¼ teaspoon of the salt. Cook stirring occasionally until the vegetables start to soften about 10 minutes. Increase the heat to moderately high. Add the chorizo and cook stirring occasionally for 2 minutes. Stir in the red pepper flakes, paprika, chicken, ½ teaspoon of the salt and the black pepper and cook stirring frequently until the chicken is almost done about 3 minutes. Cover the pan and remove from the heat.

Steam the chicken for 2 minutes. Transfer the mixture to a large glass or stainless steel bowl to cool. Boil orzo for about 10 minutes. Drain and rinse with cold water thoroughly. Add the drained orzo to the chicken mixture. Toss with the lemon juice, the remaining 2 tablespoons oil and ½ teaspoon salt, the tomato and the parsley.

Suggested pairing: Paella's Iberian roots lead us to Spain for a red Ribera Del Duero. The name literally translated as the "slopes along the Duero River" describes an area that is now the source of some of Spain's red wines. Ribera del Duero's wild cherry, herb and spice flavors will be superb with this salad.

PASTA SALAD WITH TOMATO, ARUGULA, PINE NUTS AND HERB DRESSING

Serving size = 4; cook time = 20 minutes

Ingredients
¼ c plus 3 tablespoons pine nuts
1 lb fusilli pasta
½ c cilantro leaves
½ c basil leaves
2 tsp coarsely chopped oregano leaves
1 garlic clove
¼ c mayonnaise
¼ c extra virgin olive oil
1 ½ tbsp fresh lemon juice
Kosher salt and freshly ground black pepper
2 ½ c baby arugula
1 ¼ c grape tomatoes, halved
½ sm red onion, cut into ¼ inch dice

Directions
Preheat the oven to 350 degrees. In a pie plate toast 3 tablespoons of the pine nuts until lightly golden and fragrant about 5 minutes. Set aside to cool. Boil pasta for about 10 minutes. Drain noodles and rinse with cold water. Transfer to a large bowl. Meanwhile in a food processor combine the cilantro with the basil, oregano and garlic and pulse until coarsely chopped. Add the mayonnaise, olive oil, lemon juice and the remaining ¼ cup of pine nuts and process until smooth. Season the herb dressing with salt and pepper. Toss the fusilli with the toasted pine nuts, arugula, tomatoes, red onion and the herb dressing. Season the pasta salad with salt and pepper and serve.

Suggested pairing: Herbal, lightly nutty Gavi.

THAI STYLE BEEF SALAD OVER ANGEL HAIR PASTA

Serving size = 4; cook time = 30 minutes

½ lb spaghetti
2 tbsp cooking oil
3 tbsp Asian sesame oil
½ c sliced almonds
1 jalapeno pepper, seeds and
ribs removed, minced
1 tsp minced fresh ginger
1 ½ lb ground beef
1 tsp salt
¼ c Asian fish sauce
4 scallions including green tops, chopped
1 c coarsely chopped fresh mint
¼ c lime juice (from about 2 limes), plus
1 lime, cut into wedges, for serving

Boil pasta for about 5 minutes. Drain noodles and rinse with cold water thoroughly. Toss the pasta with 1 tablespoon of the cooking oil and 2 tablespoons of the sesame oil. In a large frying pan toast the almonds over moderately low heat stirring frequently until golden brown about 5 minutes. Or toast the nuts in a 350 degrees oven for 5 to 10 minutes. Remove the nuts from the pan and chop them.

In a large frying pan heat the remaining tablespoon of cooking oil over moderately high heat. Add half the jalapeno, the ginger, beef and salt. Cook the meat stirring frequently until brown and cooked through about 10 minutes. Remove the pan from the heat and stir in the remaining tablespoon of sesame oil, the fish sauce, scallions, mint and lime juice. Put the pasta on plates and top with the beef salad. Sprinkle with the remaining minced jalapeno and the chopped almonds and serve with the lime wedges.

Suggested pairing: This dish would be a real challenge for most wines. A rich, fairly sweet and malty dark beer will make a splendid chaser.

FARFALLE WITH SPRING VEGETABLES

Serving size = 4-6; cook time = 30 minutes

Ingredients

2 slices white sandwich bread
(1 cup finely chopped)
½ c plus 2 tbsp extra virgin olive oil
2 tbsp chopped flat leaf parsley
2 tbsp snipped chives
1 tbsp chopped tarragon
Salt and freshly ground pepper
1 lb farfalle
4 tbsp unsalted butter
1 garlic clove (minced)
1 fennel bulb (halved, cored and thinly sliced)
2 scallions (thinly sliced)
1 c frozen peas, thawed, or pound
fresh peas, shelled
1 tbsp fresh lemon juice

Directions

Preheat the oven to 350 degrees. On a baking sheet toss the bread with ¼ cup of the oil and toast for 8 to 10 minutes stirring until golden. Let cool then stir in half each of the parsley, chives and tarragon. Season the crumbs with salt and pepper. In a pot of boiling salted water cook the broccolini until tender, 1 minute; using tongs transfer to a cutting board and coarsely chop. Boil pasta for about 10 minutes. Reserve 1 cup pasta water. Drain noodles and rinse with cold water.

In a deep skillet melt the butter in the remaining 6 tablespoons of oil. Add the garlic, fennel, scallions, peas and broccolini and cook over moderate heat until the fennel is crisp tender about 6 minutes. Add the pasta, lemon juice and cooking water and season with salt and pepper. Cook over moderate heat until the water is nearly absorbed. Stir in the remaining herbs. Sprinkle the pasta with the bread crumbs just before eating.

Recipe notes: The pasta can be kept at room temperature for 4 hours. The crumbs can be stored at room temperature overnight.

Suggested pairing: Zesty, herbal Sauvignon Blanc.

THAI SEAFOOD NOODLE SALAD

Serving size = 6; cook time = 1 hour

Ingredients

6 oz rice vermicelli
2 red Thai chilies, thinly sliced
2 garlic cloves, thinly sliced
¼ c sugar
½ c fresh lime juice
1/3 c Asian fish sauce
2 tbsp boiling water
½ lb med shrimp, shelled and deveined
½ lb bay scallops
½ lb sm squid, bodies cut into ½ inch rings and tentacles halved
3 plum tomatoes, seeded and diced
1 c bean sprouts
1 c mint leaves
½ sm red onion, thinly sliced
½ c salted roasted peanuts
6 butter lettuce leaves, for serving
Cilantro leaves, for garnish

Directions

In a medium bowl cover the vermicelli in cold water and soak for 30 minutes. Meanwhile in a mortar pound the Thai chilies and garlic to a paste with 1 tablespoon of the sugar. Add the lime juice, fish sauce, boiling water and the remaining 3 tablespoons of sugar and pound until sugar dissolves. Let the dressing stand at room temperature for 30 minutes. Bring a large saucepan of water to a boil. Fill a bowl with ice water. Add the shrimp to the boiling water and cook until white throughout and curled, 2 to 3 minutes.

Using a slotted spoon transfer the shrimp to the ice water. Add the scallops to the boiling water and cook until white and firm, 2 to 3 minutes. Transfer the scallops to the ice water. Add the squid to the boiling water and cook just until firm about 45 seconds. Transfer the squid to the ice water. Drain all of the seafood and pat dry. Bring a fresh saucepan of water to a boil and refill the bowl with ice water. Drain the vermicelli and add to the boiling water. Cook just until al dente, 1 minute.

Drain and transfer to the ice water. Drain again and pat dry. Cut the vermicelli into 3 inch lengths. In a large bowl toss the seafood with the vermicelli, tomatoes, bean sprouts, mint, red onion, peanuts and chile dressing. Arrange the lettuce leaves on a platter and fill with the seafood salad. Garnish with cilantro leaves and serve.

Recipe notes: All of the components can be prepared up to 1 day ahead and refrigerated separately. Toss the salad just before serving.

Suggested pairing: Citrusy dry Washington state Riesling.

BOW TIE SALAD WITH SCALLOPS, BLACK OLIVES, ORANGES AND MINT

Serving size = 4; cook time = 25 minutes

Ingredients

¾ lb bow tie pasta
1 lb sea scallops
¾ tsp salt
¼ tsp fresh-ground black pepper
5 tbsp olive oil
2 navel oranges
1 tbsp lemon juice
½ c Kalamata or other black olives, pitted
½ sm red onion, chopped fine
6 tbsp chopped fresh mint

Directions

Boil pasta for about 10 minutes. Drain noodles and rinse with cold water thoroughly. Meanwhile season the scallops with ¼ teaspoon of the salt and 1/8 teaspoon of the pepper. In a large nonstick frying pan heat 1 tablespoon of the oil over moderately high heat. Sear the scallops in two batches if necessary until brown and just done 1 to 2 minutes per side. Let cool.

Using a stainless steel knife peel the oranges down to the flesh removing all of the white pith. Cut the sections away from the membranes and put them in a large glass or stainless steel bowl. Squeeze the juice from the membranes into the bowl. Add the remaining 4 tablespoons oil, the lemon juice, olives, onion, mint and the remaining ½ teaspoon salt and 1/8 teaspoon pepper. Stir to combine. Add the pasta and scallops and stir again.

Suggested pairing: A white or rose wine from Provence or the Languedoc Roussillon region of France makes sense with this; either will pair well with the mint and the salty olive tastes of the dish.

SMOKED SALMON MACARONI SALAD WITH SPINACH, LEMON AND GOAT CHEESE

Serving size = 2-3; cook time = 15 minutes

Ingredients
3 ½ oz macaroni (1 cup)
¼ c mayonnaise
2 tbsp freshly squeezed lemon juice
½ tsp freshly ground pepper
1 garlic clove, finely minced
2 oz smoked salmon (not lox; ¼ cup)
2 oz goat cheese
3 thin slices of lemon, cut into 16 slivers each
1 c roughly chopped spinach
Sea salt

Directions
Boil pasta for about 10 minutes. Drain noodles and rinse with cold water. In a medium bowl whisk together the mayonnaise, freshly squeezed lemon juice, freshly ground pepper and garlic. Add the macaroni, smoked salmon, goat cheese, lemon slivers and the spinach to the bowl. Toss to coat evenly with the dressing then season with sea salt.

ASIAN PASTA SALAD WITH SESAME GINGER DRESSING

Serving size = 6; cook time = 20 minutes

Ingredients

For the Dressing

¼ c seasoned rice wine vinegar
1 tsp ginger, grated
2 cloves garlic, minced
1 tsp Sriracha
1 tbsp soy sauce
3 tbsp pure honey
3 tsp granulated sugar
2 tbsp Asian toasted sesame oil (caramel brown in color)
1/3 c canola or olive oil
¼ tsp kosher salt
½ tsp fresh ground black pepper
1 tbsp toasted sesame seeds

For Pasta Salad

16 oz cooked rotini, drained and cooled (sprinkle with olive oil to prevent sticking)
16 oz bag of fresh cole slaw mix (no dressing)
1 red bell pepper, seeded and thinly sliced
½ c edamame (pre shelled)
¼ c thinly sliced green onion
¼ c chopped cilantro
¼ c toasted sliced almonds

Directions

Do ahead in a bowl; whisk together all dressing ingredients until well blended. Transfer to desired container and keep chilled until ready to use. When ready to serve toss together all salad ingredients except for almonds in a serving bowl. Gently toss in desired amounts of dressing. Garnish with almonds and serve.

Recipe notes: Unused dressing can be kept in an airtight container for several weeks in the fridge. Make the recipe by using your favorite gluten free pasta. This version is meatless, but feel free to add shredded cooked chicken or shrimp if desired.

PUTTANESCA PASTA SALAD

Serving size = 4-5; cook time = 20 minutes

Ingredients

3 c uncooked dry rotini pasta
3 tbsp extra virgin olive oil
1 med red onion minced
3 cloves garlic minced
6 c large tomatoes diced (about 4)
1 tsp brown sugar
2/3 c pitted Kalamata olives
1 red pepper diced optional
½ tsp chili flakes or 2 tbsp hot sauce optional
1 tsp anchovy paste optional
3 tbsp chopped capers optional
¼ c extra virgin olive oil
3 tbsp balsamic vinegar
¼ c chopped fresh basil

Directions

Boil pasta for about 10 minutes. Drain noodles and rinse with cold water. Meanwhile in a large sauté pan heat the olive oil over medium heat. Add the garlic and onions and sauté for about 1 minute or 2 until the onion soften but do not brown. Turn heat to high and toss in the olives, tomatoes, brown sugar, chili flakes, anchovy paste and capers and cook until the tomatoes just start to break down.

Add the red pepper and basil and cook for an additional few minutes until the juice from the tomatoes has mostly cooked off. Season the sauce with salt and pepper to taste. Remove from the heat and stir in the ¼ cup olive oil and the balsamic vinegar. Toss the sauce with the cooked pasta and chopped basil. Whether serving this salad hot or cold you can still serve it with a sprinkle of finely grated parmesan cheese if you like.

BEST OF THE OLIVE BAR PASTA SALAD

Serving size = 6-8; cook time = 20 minutes

Ingredients

¼ c red wine vinegar
2 tbsp fresh oregano leaves, chopped
4 tsp Dijon mustard
2 tsp lemon zest plus 1 tablespoon fresh lemon juice (from 1 lemon)
2 med garlic cloves, grated on a Microplane grater
½ tsp black pepper
½ c olive oil
12 oz orecchiette pasta, cooked according to package directions
1 c cherry tomatoes, halved
1 c loosely packed fresh basil leaves, torn
7 oz feta cheese, cubed
½ c sun dried tomatoes, sliced
½ c Castelvetrano olives, pitted
½ c Kalamata olives, pitted
2 tbsp drained capers

Directions

Whisk together vinegar, oregano, mustard, lemon zest and juice, garlic, and black pepper in a large bowl. Add olive oil in a slow steady stream whisking constantly until smooth. Add cooked pasta, cherry tomatoes, basil, feta, sun dried tomatoes, olives and capers, and toss gently to combine. Serve at room temperature or chilled.

QUICK AND EASY PASTA SALAD

Serving size = 10; cook time = 20 minutes

Ingredients

Pasta Salad

1 lb dried fusilli pasta
1 c sliced bell pepper (1 medium)
1 c thinly sliced zucchini (1/2 medium)
1 c halved cherry tomatoes
1/3 c thinly sliced scallions (5 to 6)
¼ c sliced pepperoncini or banana peppers, optional
1 c (4 oz) halved mixed olives
1 c (2 oz) grated parmesan cheese or hard cheese
1 c (6 oz) fresh mozzarella balls, chopped
1/3 c fresh parsley or basil, optional

Homemade Dressing

1/3 c red wine vinegar, white wine vinegar or champagne vinegar
½ tsp fine sea salt, plus more to taste
½ tsp fresh ground black pepper
½ tsp dried oregano
2 to 3 tablespoons juice from pepperoncini jar, optional
½ c extra virgin olive oil

Directions

Boil pasta for about 10 minutes. Drain noodles and rinse with cold water. In the bottom of a large bowl make the dressing. Whisk the red wine vinegar, salt, pepper, oregano, pepperoncini juice (if using), and the olive oil until blended. Add the drained and rinsed pasta to the dressing and mix well.

Stir in the bell pepper, zucchini, tomatoes, scallions, pepperoncini (if using), olives, parmesan, mozzarella, and the herbs (if using). Taste for seasoning and adjust with salt and pepper as needed. Serve or for the best results cover and refrigerate at least 30 minutes and up to 5 days.

BROCCOLINI AND SWEET PEPPER PASTA SALAD

Serving size = 4-5; cook time = 20 minutes

Ingredients

5 oz dried rotini pasta
3 c cut up broccolini or small broccoli florets
3 tbsp white balsamic vinegar
2 tbsp canola oil
2 tbsp honey
2 cloves garlic, minced
¼ tsp crushed red pepper, optional
1 lrg red sweet pepper, cut
into bite - size strips
½ c chopped red onion
¼ c sliced almonds, toasted
¼ c chopped fresh basil
2 oz goat cheese, crumbled

Directions

Boil pasta for about 10 minutes. Add the broccolini and cook for 3 minutes more or until pasta is done. Drain and run under cold water to cool completely. Drain again. Meanwhile in a large bowl whisk together the vinegar, oil, honey, garlic and crushed red pepper if using. Add the pasta mixture, sweet pepper, onion, almonds, and basil to the vinegar mixture. Toss to combine. Gently stir in cheese. Season to taste.

SICILIAN PASTA SALAD

Serving size = 2; cook time = 2 hours 20 minutes

Ingredients

12 oz penne pasta
1/3 c olive oil
2 cloves garlic minced
1 med onion diced
½ red bell pepper diced
1 tbsp tomato pasta
¼ c water
4 tbsp white wine
1 tbsp fresh parsley minced
1 tsp fresh rosemary minced
¼ fresh thyme minced
¼ fresh oregano minced
1 tbsp fresh basil minced, plus a handful of small leaves for garnishing
1 tsp sea salt
1/8 tsp black pepper freshly ground
½ c zucchini diced
½ c green beans chopped 1 inch pieces
¼ c sun dried tomatoes chopped
1-12 oz jar marinated artichoke hearts drained and chopped
1 6 oz whole black pitted olives drained
½ c Asiago or pecorino cheese grated

Directions

Boil pasta for about 10 minutes. Drain noodles and rinse with cold water. Toss in 1 teaspoon of olive oil. Set aside. Heat a large skillet to medium high heat and add the remaining olive oil. Mix in the garlic, onion, and bell pepper. Sauté for 3 to 4 minutes or until the vegetables are tender. In a small bowl combine the tomato, pasta and water. Mix well. Add the tomato puree, wine, fresh herbs and seasonings to the skillet. Continue to simmer for 5 to 7 minutes. Add the zucchini and green beans and cook for a few minutes until softened. Remove from heat.

Mix in the sun dried tomatoes, artichoke hearts and olives. Add the pasta and stir until everything is well combined. Chill completely for about 2 hours before mixing in the cheese and garnishing with the basil leaves. Serve.

Recipe notes: If this is a make ahead dish that will be in the refrigerator for more than a couple hours wait to combine the final ingredients. Chill the penne, cooked vegetable mixture, basil leaves and grated cheese separately. 30 minutes before serving toss the pasta, vegetable mixture and cheese together. Garnish with the basil leaves. Serve cold.

SUMMER VEGETABLE ORZO SALAD

Serving size = 4-6; cook time = 25 minutes

Ingredients

Salad:

1 c uncooked orzo
¾ c fresh or frozen corn, (if using fresh I recommend grilling it)
1 c cherry tomatoes, halved
2 peaches, diced
1 jalapeno, deseeded and minced
2 green onions, finely sliced
1 tbsp fresh finely chopped basil
Kosher salt and fresh ground black pepper to taste

Dressing:

2 tbsp fresh lime juice
2 tsp olive oil
2 ½ tsp honey or agave nectar
½ tsp ground cumin
¼ tsp granulated garlic
Kosher salt and fresh ground black pepper to taste

Directions

Boil orzo for about 8-10 minutes. Drain and rinse with cold water. Add the orzo to a large serving bowl along with the remaining salad ingredients. In a small bowl whisk together the dressing ingredients then pour it onto the salad. Toss everything together and taste for seasoning. Serve immediately or cover and refrigerate until ready to serve.

POPPY SEED CHICKEN AND GRAPE PASTA SALAD

Serving size = 6-8; cook time = 40 minutes

Ingredients

10 oz bow tie pasta (about 4 cups)
2 c cooked and cooled, diced chicken breast (I used rotisserie)
12 oz red grapes halved (about 2 cups)
1 c diced celery
¾ c Fisher Sliced Almonds
½ c sliced green onions green portion
1/3 c dried cranberries (optional)Dressing
½ c fat free plain Greek Yogurt
½ c full fat mayonnaise
3 tbsp white wine vinegar or apple cider vinegar
3 tbsp honey
2 tbsp granulated sugar
1 ½ tbsp. poppy seeds
½ salt then more to taste

Directions

Boil pasta for about 10 minutes. Drain noodles and rinse with cold water. Set aside and let cool. In a mixing bowl whisk together Greek yogurt, mayonnaise, vinegar, honey, sugar, poppy seeds and ½ salt. Add drained pasta to a salad bowl along with chicken, grapes, celery, almonds, green onions and cranberries. Pour dressing over top and toss to evenly coat. Season with more salt to taste and toss. Chill at least 30 minutes (and up to 1 day) before serving (this allows some time for the pasta to absorb the dressing and time for the flavors to meld). Serve chilled.

Recipe notes: Don't leave out the almonds: For this recipe I used Fisher Sliced Almonds and they are a key ingredient here. I love that they are preserved free and I also love the resealable packaging that helps them stay fresh. We like to snack on them plus we add them to so many things. I love that they are thinly sliced so you get that perfect thin bite with each piece for multiple layers of crunch!

TUNA PASTA SALAD

Serving size = 5; cook time = 15 minutes

Ingredients

8 oz small shell pasta
7 oz canned albacore white tuna,
packed in water, drained
2 ribs celery, chopped
¼ cup red onion, chopped
1 c frozen peas
½ c mayonnaise
½ c plain Greek yogurt
Dried dill weed, to taste, optional
Salt and freshly ground black pepper, to taste

Directions

Boil pasta for about 10 minutes. Drain noodles and rinse with cold water. In a large bowl add chopped onion and celery, peas, cooked pasta and drained tuna. In a separate bowl mix the mayo and Greek yogurt. Stir half of the sauce into the pasta mixture and toss to evenly coat. Season with salt and pepper and dried dill to taste.

Recipe notes: This tuna pasta salad with shell noodles, peas, tuna, celery and Greek yogurt is fast, healthy and a dish your whole family can enjoy!

SUN DRIED TOMATO, WHITE BEAN AND GOAT CHEESE PASTA SALAD

Serving size = 8; cook time = 25 minutes

Ingredients

½ c extra virgin olive oil
1 c fresh basil
2 fresh chives
2 sprigs fresh dill
2 tbsp lemon juice
1 tbsp red wine vinegar
1 clove garlic, smashed
½ tsp crushed red pepper flakes or more to taste
Kosher salt

Salad

1 lb gemelli pasta
1 bunch asparagus cut into 1 inch pieces
4-6 oz soft goat cheese, crumbled
1 jar (8 oz) oil packed sun dried tomatoes, chopped
1 can (14 oz) white beans, drained
1 avocado, sliced

Directions

To make the vinaigrette. In a blender combine the olive oil, basil, chives, dill, lemon juice, vinegar, garlic, 1 teaspoon of the salt and a pinch of red pepper flakes until smooth. Taste and adjust salt as needed. Boil pasta for about 10 minutes. During the last 2 to 3 minutes of cooking add the asparagus to the water. Drain noodles and rinse with hot water.

In a large bowl toss the hot pasta and asparagus with the goat cheese and a couple large spoonful's of the basil vinaigrette. Toss well until the goat cheese coats the pasta completely. Add the sun dried tomatoes and white beans tossing to combine. Top the pasta with avocado. Serve the remaining vinaigrette on the side.

Recipe notes: A simple colorful pasta salad that's perfect for lunches, picnics, BBQ's and easy dinners. Fresh pasta tossed with homemade basil vinaigrette, creamy goat cheese, sun dried tomatoes, white beans and finished with sliced avocado. This is a mayo free pasta salad that everyone will love.

STRAWBERRY AVOCADO PASTA SALAD

Serving size = 8; cook time = 20 minutes

Ingredients

16 oz uncooked penne pasta
1 tbsp salt
2 c baby arugula
Salt and pepper to taste
1 lb strawberries, hulled and sliced
2 avocados, cubed
1 c feta cheese, crumbled
½ c chopped fresh basil
1 tbsp lemon juice
½ c poppy seed dressing
½ c greek yogurt

Directions

Boil pasta for about 10 minutes. Drain noodles and rinse with hot water. Return to pot. While still hot stir in the arugula allowing it to wilt. Stir in the salt and pepper to taste. Add in the sliced strawberries, cubed avocado and feta cheese. In a separate small bowl whisk together the lemon juice, poppy seed dressing and greek yogurt until smooth. Pour dressing over the still warm pasta and stir to full coat/combine. Serve warm or cold. Brighten with a bit more lemon juice.

Recipe notes: Strawberry avocado pasta salad is an easy and tasty summer pasta salad recipe that everyone will love. This penne pasta salad with feta, strawberries, avocado, poppy seed dressing and more is so light and fresh. Serve it warm or serve it cold either way it's sure to be a hit and the strawberries make it really good.

BUFFALO CHICKEN PASTA SALAD

Serving size = 8; cook time = 26 minutes

Ingredients

2 c rotini pasta

1 chicken breast, cooked and shredded, about 1 cup

4 stalks celery, chopped, about 1 cup

1 c shredded carrots

½ c bottled ranch dressing

2 tbsp buffalo sauce, more to taste, I used Frank's

2 tbsp crumbled blue cheese

Directions

Mix together the ranch, blue cheese and buffalo sauce in a small bowl and set aside. Test the spiciness of the dressing and add more hot sauce to taste. Toss the cooked and cooled rotini, shredded chicken, celery and carrots together in a large bowl. Pour dressing over the pasta and stir until evenly coated. Divide into bowls and serve.

Recipe notes: Pre-cook your noodles and have all ingredients chopped and ready to go in the fridge. A few minutes before serving dump all ingredients in one bowl and top with dressing.

RAINBOW ANTIPASTO PASTA SALAD

Serving size = 6-8; cook time = 20 minutes

Ingredients

1 lb dry rotini pasta
4 - 6 c chopped antipasto ingredients, (I used diced salami, mozzarella, cherry tomatoes, olives, artichoke hearts, pepperoncini, roasted red peppers)
1 c chopped fresh kale, massaged
Quarter of a small red onion, peeled and thinly sliced
1 batch italian herb vinaigrette

Italian herb vinaigrette ingredients

1/3 c extra virgin olive oil
¼ c red wine vinegar
2 tsp italian blend herb grinder italian seasoning or homemade
½ tsp kosher salt
½ tsp freshly cracked black pepper
¼ tsp garlic powder

Directions

Antipasto pasta salad

Boil pasta for about 10 minutes. Drain noodles and rinse with cold water until no longer hot. In a large bowl combine the cooked pasta, antipasto ingredients, kale and onion. Drizzle the italian herb vinaigrette on top then toss to combine. Serve immediately or cover and refrigerate for up to 3 days.

Italian herb vinaigrette

Whisk all ingredients together until combined. *Recipe notes:* This salad is the perfect way to use up leftover antipasto ingredients. Plus it's easy to make tossed with a zesty italian herb vinaigrette and absolutely delicious. To soften the kale I placed it in the mixing bowl first along with 2 tablespoons of the vinaigrette and then used my hands to massage the vinaigrette into the kale for about 1 minute. This makes it considerably softer and will turn the kale a nice dark green color.

BACON RANCH PASTA SALAD

Serving size = 6; cook time = 20 minutes

Ingredients

1 pkg 12 oz rotini pasta
½ c mayonnaise
½ c sour cream
1 pkg 1 oz dry ranch dressing mix
½ tsp garlic powder
½ c milk
8 slices cooked bacon, chopped
1 lrg tomato, chopped
1 can 4.25 oz sliced black olives, drained
1 c shredded cheddar cheese

Directions

Boil pasta for about 10 minutes. Drain noodles and rinse with cold water. Set aside. In a large bowl whisk together the mayonnaise, sour cream, dry ranch mix, garlic powder and milk. Add pasta, cooked bacon pieces, tomato, olives and cheese to the bowl. Gently toss to combine everything. Cover and chill in refrigerator at least 2 hours before serving.

Recipe notes: Tender pasta is coated in creamy ranch dressing, bacon and lots of other goodies in the bacon ranch pasta salad. This pasta salad is perfect for summer barbecues and is always a hit. Oscar Meyer packages of precooked bacon pieces to save on time is a great alternative. When ready to serve you can toss with a little extra milk if it seems to dry.

ASIAN PASTA SALAD

Serving size = 4; cook time = 20 minutes

Ingredients
1 (8 oz) package spaghetti
1 tsp olive oil
6 tbsp soy sauce
¼ c white sugar
3 tbsp rice vinegar
1 tbsp toasted sesame seeds
2 tsp sweet chili sauce
1 tsp sesame oil
2 green onions, chopped
1 red bell pepper, chopped (optional)
1 c sugar snap peas (optional)

Directions
Boil pasta for about 10 minutes. Drain noodles and rinse with cold water. Transfer pasta to a serving bowl and toss with olive oil. Whisk soy sauce, sugar, vinegar, sesame seeds, chili sauce and sesame oil together in a bowl until sugar dissolves. Toss soy sauce mixture with pasta; top with green onions, red bell pepper and snap peas. Refrigerate 30 minutes to overnight to allow flavors to blend. Toss again before serving.

TUSCAN PASTA SALAD

Serving size = 6; cook time = 20 minutes

Ingredients

16 oz bow tie pasta cooked and
drained in cold water
1-7 oz jar sun dried tomatoes in oil drained
1 red bell pepper diced
1-6.5 oz can sliced olives
1 c spinach
¼ c basil chopped
½ c grated parmesan cheese

Dressing

¾ c olive oil
2 tbsp white vinegar
2 tbsp water
1 tsp salt
1 tsp sugar
1 tsp dry oregano
1 tsp dry basil
1 clove garlic
Black pepper to taste

Directions

In a large bowl combine pasta, sundried tomatoes, bell pepper, olives, spinach, basil and parmesan cheese. Toss until combined. In a small bowl whisk olive oil, vinegar, water, salt, sugar, oregano, basil, garlic and salt and pepper. Drizzle the dressing over the pasta salad and serve.

Recipe notes: Tuscan pasta salad is an easy pasta salad with sun dried tomatoes, peppers, spinach and olives tossed in a tangy dressing. This pasta salad is perfect for your next potluck!

DEVILED EGG MACARONI SALAD

Serving size = 8; cook time = 20 minutes

Ingredients

16 oz Ditalini pasta
1 ½ c mayonnaise
2 tbsp sour cream
2 tbsp mustard
2 tbsp sweet pickle relish
6 hardboiled eggs
2 - 3 ribs celery finely, chopped
½ c black olives, sliced
4 oz jar pimientos, drained
3 tbsp fresh dill, chopped
1 tsp paprika
Salt and pepper to taste
Garnish with green onions

Directions

Boil pasta for about 10 minutes. Drain noodles and rinse with cold water. Prepare hard boiled eggs, let cool and slice. In a large mixing bowl combine all the ingredients except eggs and mix with pasta until blended. Gently fold in eggs. Garnish with green onions. Chill until ready to serve.

Recipe notes: This deviled egg macaroni salad is creamy and loaded with hard boiled eggs. Quick and delicious and the perfect addition to any mean.

MEXICAN STREET CORN PASTA SALAD

Serving size = 10; cook time = 20 minutes

Ingredients

16 oz rotini pasta
Olive oil for tossing pasta
2 (15 oz) cans corn, drained
½ c cotija or queso fresco cheese
3 tbsp freshly chopped cilantro
plus more for garnish
1 c sour cream
2/3 c mayonnaise
½ tsp garlic powder
Zest and juice of 2 limes
1 tsp chili powder
1 couple pinches cayenne pepper
Kosher salt
Fresh cracked pepper

Directions

Boil pasta for about 10 minutes. Drain noodles and rinse with cold water. Toss with olive oil, salt, and pepper and set aside to cool to room temperature or pop in the fridge to speed up the cooling process. In a medium bowl combine sour cream, mayo, lime zest and juice, garlic powder, chili powder, cayenne pepper and a couple large pinches of salt and pepper. Add pasta, corn, cotija and cilantro to a large bowl. Pour most of the dressing over the pasta and toss until everything is well coated. Transfer to serving platter. Drizzle with remaining dressing and garnish with fresh chopped cilantro.

Recipe notes: This Mexican street corn pasta salad is loaded with corn, cotija and a deliciously tangy, creamy dressing that is the stuff dreams are made of. It's quick and easy to throw together and is made up of mostly pantry ingredients that you've probably already have in your kitchen. The dressing in this pasta salad will thicken as it sits. I would recommend dressing it just before serving or it you'll be enjoying this pasta salad a few hours after you make it, feel free to add a splash of lime juice or even milk to loosen things up.

Directions
Boil pasta for about 10 minutes. Drain and rinse with cold water. Set aside. In a small bowl whisk together olive oil and balsamic vinegar then season with salt and pepper. To the bowl add pasta, garlic and tomatoes; toss with dressing to combine. Garnish with basil and serve.

BRUSETTA PASTA SALAD

Serving size = 4; cook time = 20 minutes

Ingredients
1 lb orecchiette
¼ c extra virgin olive oil
1 tbsp balsamic vinegar
Kosher salt
Freshly ground black pepper
1 clove garlic, minced
1 pt cherry tomatoes, preferably multi colored, halved
¼ c torn basil, for garnish

CHICKEN CEASAR PASTA SALAD

Serving size = 8; cook time = 35 minutes

Ingredients

1 cup mayonnaise
1/3 cup sour cream
1 clove large garlic pressed
2 tbsp lemon juice
2 anchovies finely minced
1 tsp Worcestershire sauce
1 lb penne pasta, cooked until al dente and rinsed with cool water
6 leaves large Romaine lettuce, thinly sliced
1 ½ c grape tomatoes
4 green onions, green parts sliced
½ c finely shredded Parmesan cheese
½ tsp ground black pepper
2 grilled chicken breasts, diced
1 ½ c croutons

Directions

In a small bowl stir together the mayonnaise and the Worcestershire sauce. Toss half of the dressing with the pasta and refrigerate for 30 minutes. Mix in remaining ingredients including the remaining dressing and serve.

Recipe notes: One of my favorite ways to break out of a pasta rut is to make pasta salad modeled after one of America's favorite salads. Cobb pasta salad and greek pasta salad are two favorites. I'm almost always pleased with the outcome probably because there are so few ingredients or flavors that I don't like with pasta. Pasta is like a blank canvas you can use to let your creativity run free. I like to mix half of the dressing with the pasta and chill it and then mix in the remaining dressing just before serving but you can do it all at once. Be sure to salt your cooking water for the pasta well at least 1 tablespoon of salt. Anchovies can be omitted. You might want to double the Worcestershire sauce if you do.

CREAMY CHEDDAR MACARONI SALAD

Serving size = 4; cook time = 1 hour

Ingredients

1 c elbow macaroni
¾ c cheddar cheese, cubed
1 stalk celery, sliced
½ sm green bell pepper, chopped
½ c frozen peas, thawed
1/3 c onion, chopped
¼ c mayonnaise or ¼ cup salad dressing
¼ c sour cream
2 tbsp milk
2 tbsp sweet pickle relish

Directions

Boil pasta for about 10 minutes. Drain noodles and rinse with cold water. In a mixing bowl combine cooked macaroni, cheese, celery, green bell pepper, peas and onion. Stir gently to combine. For dressing: Mix mayonnaise or salad dressing, sour cream, milk and pickle relish and ¼ teaspoon salt. Toss dressing with macaroni mixture. Cover and chill for 4 to 24 hours. If necessary stir in a small amount of additional milk.

BARBECUE RANCH PASTA SALAD

Serving size = 6-8; cook time = 30 minutes

Ingredients

1 lb pasta, I used cavatappi,
cooked until al dente
1 c hidden valley honey bb1 dressing
1/3 c sour cream
1 c black beans, rinsed and drained
1 c canned corn, drained
½ red bell pepper, diced
½ sm red onion, finely diced
1 - ½ c diced cooked chicken
1 c shredded cheddar cheese
2 tbsp chopped fresh cilantro
1 c corn chips

Directions

Place cooked pasta in a large bowl. Stir together hidden valley honey bbq dressing and sour cream and pour over pasta. Toss to mix. Add all remaining ingredients except corn chips, and stir to combine. Refrigerate until ready to serve and sprinkle corn chips on top just before serving.

Recipe notes: BBQ ranch pasta salad is sure to become a picnic favorite. It's creamy and full of smoky flavor from hidden valley ranch honey bbq dressing.

JALAPENO POPPER MACARONI SALAD

Serving size = 4-5; cook time = 30 minutes

Ingredients

Roasted Jalapenos

5 large jalapenos (tops, seeds and veins removed)
Olive oil
Salt/pepper

Macaroni Salad

8 oz dry elbow macaroni, cooked according to package instructions
2 oz cream cheese, softened and cubed
6 – 8 oz bacon, cooked and chopped
4 oz mild cheddar cheese, cut into small cubes
1/3 c mayonnaise
¼ c sour cream
½ tsp garlic powder
¼ tsp onion powder
Ground pepper, to taste

Directions

Roasted Jalapenos

Preheat oven to 425 degrees. Toss jalapenos with just enough olive oil to lightly coat. Sprinkle with salt and pepper. Roast jalapeno's on a rimmed baking sheet for 10 minutes. Let cool then chop.

Macaroni salad

Mix cooked macaroni and cream cheese while pasta is still slightly warm. Let cool then add bacon, cheddar, mayo, sour cream, garlic powder, onion powder, pepper and jalapenos. Store in refrigerator in airtight container until served.

Recipe notes: Just in time for barbecue season, this jalapeno popper macaroni salad recipe makes a fantastic side dish. Your favorite pasta salad made with cheddar, bacon and roasted jalapenos for a fun twist. Pack it up in a cooker and take a family picnic.

COLD PEANUT NOODLE SALAD

Serving size = 6; cook time = 30 minutes

Ingredients

6 oz dry linguine noodles
4 c mix of cabbage, carrots and radish, shredded or grated
1 red bell pepper, finely sliced
3 scallions, sliced
½ bunch cilantro, chopped (or sub basil and mint)
1 tbsp, or less, jalapeno, finely chopped
¼ - ½ c roasted, crushed peanuts, garnish

Thai peanut sauce

3 thin slices ginger – cut across the grain, about the size of a quarter.
1 fat clove garlic
¼ c peanut butter or sub almond butter
¼ c fresh orange juice, roughly ½ and orange
3 tablespoon fresh lime juice, 1 lime
2 tablespoons soy sauce
3 tablespoon honey or agave
3 tablespoon toasted sesame oil
½ - teaspoon cayenne pepper
½ teaspoon salt
Sesame ginger tofu, optional

Directions

Cook noodles: Boil pasta for about 10 minutes. Drain noodles and rinse with cold water.
Blend the peanut sauce: While noodles are cooking blend the peanut sauce ingredients together using a blender until smooth. *Toss:* Place shredded veggies, bell pepper, scallions, cilantro and jalapeno into a serving bowl and toss. Add the cold noodles to the serving bowl and toss again. Pour the peanut sauce over top and toss well to combine. *Taste*: Adjust the salt

and add chili flakes if you want. You can garnish with cilantro and lime wedge for an extra kick.

Recipe notes: This is a simple delicious recipe for Thai Noodle Salad with Peanut Sauce, loaded up with healthy veggies. Vegan and Gluten free, this make ahead salad is perfect for midweek lunches or large gathering. Add sesame ginger tofu for added protein.

obtained

3

9 781489 740892